D0341496

Crossroads
at Midlife

Crossroads at Midlife

Your Aging Parents, Your Emotions,
and Your Self

Frances Cohen Praver

Foreword by Irwin Hirsch

Westport, Connecticut
London

Library of Congress Cataloging-in-Publication Data

Praver, Frances Cohen, 1937–
   Crossroads at midlife : your aging parents, your emotions, and your self /
Frances Cohen Praver ; foreword by Irwin Hirsch.
      p. cm.
   Includes bibliographical references and index.
   ISBN 0-275-98183-5 (alk. paper)
   1. Aging parents—Care. 2. Adult children of aging parents—Family
relationships. 3. Caregivers. 4. Intergenerational relations. I. Title.
HQ1063.6.P73 2004
   306.874—dc22   2004043699

British Library Cataloging in Publication Data is available.

Library of Congress Catalog Card Number: 2004043699
ISBN: 0-275-98183-5

First published in 2004

Praeger Publishers, 88 Post Road West, Westport, CT 06881
An imprint of Greenwood Publishing Group, Inc.
www.praeger.com

Printed in the United States of America

The paper used in this book complies with the
Permanent Paper Standard issued by the National
Information Standards Organization (Z39.48-1984)

10 9 8 7 6 5 4 3 2

To the memory of my parents Bessie and Sam,
and the presence of my two men,
my husband Bob and my son Leland

Contents

Foreword

Dr. Frances Cohen Praver has written an important book for a wide audience. It is a book about a phase of life that so many of us, in and out of the helping professions, are facing in a volume never seen in previous generations. As people live longer they face a myriad of serious problems that earlier and more sudden deaths had mitigated. Longer life is a very mixed blessing. On the one hand, there are obvious virtues—wisdom accumulated, passed down, and applied to interests and relationships, and the potential to share the wonderful riches of having born children, grandchildren, and even great-grandchildren. On the other hand, living longer often means living with much physical/and or mental infirmity and pain, enduring great physical and emotional stressors that early and/or sudden death relieved one from.

In this context, perhaps the greatest downside of longer life is the stress that it places on one's children, children who by default become parents to their own parents, while simultaneously negotiating the other difficulties of middle age, including caring for actual children. This is the population most directly addressed by Dr. Praver, in her effort as a psychologist and psychoanalyst, to both articulate the problems and aid those in the midst of what has become for many an acute contemporary dilemma.

Most of those in middle age grew up expecting to reap the fruits of hard work and to pass on to their children the accumulated personal and emotional riches. Caring for one's aging and increasingly infirm parents has added a whole new dimension of worry and responsibility to this period of life. Such responsibility can produce enormous emotional and practical conflict between selfish pursuit of pleasure and self-sacrifice; attention to one's spouse or lovers and the often wrenching emotional engagement with one's parents, the needs of one's children and those of dependent parents and siblings who somehow manage to feel free of responsibility for parents and those who are committed or burdened by those same responsibilities. It is not infrequent that individuals residing in this difficult mid-life period wrestle with the often horrible wish that their parents die and thereby make room for the freedom to pursue a life of greater pleasure. Resentment of burden and guilt in relation to this can be crippling, and cast a huge shadow over a period of life originally anticipated to be oriented toward reaping some of the rewards of hard work and commitment to children during their young and demanding years.

Viewing the often slow and gradual deterioration and demise of one's parents, in addition, offers a jarring preview of what is to come for us in middle age. This can be a frightening forecast, and it has the power to depress. Of course, the ultimate death of parents places the adult child directly next in line, a stark but necessary confrontation with one's mortality.

Dr. Praver both eloquently describes what I all too briefly summarized and offers helpful ways to deal with the last half, third, or quarter of life. In the face of painful and dire experience, she uses her clinical acumen to remain upbeat, optimistic, and pragmatically useful, while not minimizing enormous difficulty. With liberal use of examples from her clinical practice, Dr. Praver illustrates not only useful ways to cope with adversity and human suffering, but means by which one can actually grow stronger from such experience. This book shares the wisdom of an experienced professional in facing profound matters of life and death, and at the same time translates this wisdom into highly readable and practical form for professionals and lay audiences alike.

Irwin Hirsch
Professor of Psychology and Supervisor,
Postdoctoral Program in Psychoanalysis,
Adelphi University, New York
Distinguished Visiting Faculty,
William Alanson White Institue, New York

Acknowledgments

I am a fortunate woman. I have encountered remarkable people without whom this leg of my journey would not be possible. As a mature adult, I returned to school to get my doctorate in clinical psychology, after which I completed four years of additional study and obtained my postdoctorate degree in psychoanalysis at Adelphi University. Upon entering the postdoctoral program at Adelphi University, I found an inviting, warm, and well-functioning family. The professors were dedicated, informative, and only too eager to share their theoretical and clinical expertise. They taught me the art of psychoanalysis along with the art of using my self in its entirety as an instrument in my work. Irwin Hirsch, PhD, has been a fount of erudite thinking and creativity and an inspirational force. His work on relational analysis has added clarity and depth to my work. Gladys Guarton, PhD, has a way of weaving cutting edge theories with psychoanalysis that is unique. She introduced me to novel ideas that added richness and dimension to my work. I owe much to the Adelphi group.

Roberta Jelinek, PhD, an analyst, was my therapist. She continues to be my role model as a professional and, most important, as a woman. Dr. Jellinek is the paradigm of grace, empathy, and wit. My good friends and colleagues, Julia Becker, MD, and Bob Reich, MD, spent many long hours into the night discussing cases with me. They are both talented clinicians and kind people, and I learned a lot from them.

Mary Sue Seymour, my agent, has been my angel. Her positive outlook and faith in my work were motivating influences. The expertise and encouragement of my editor, Debbie Carvalko, have moved the work forward.

The caring and love of my sister Dorothy have bolstered me in a way that only a sister can. My son Leland has let me know how proud he is of me, as I am of him. My aging process is made so much richer by his loving, artistic, and intellectual presence. My beloved husband Bob has been there for me from the beginning of my transition. His love, generosity, and faith in me have helped me realize my dreams.

My parents Bessie and Sam were my producers. My mother's uncanny intuition and my father's moral imagination continue to have a strong internal presence. They affect all facets of my life.

Finally, I learn daily from my patients, who assist my development as a psychoanalyst and writer.

Introduction

I am often asked why I wrote this book. The answer is simple—my awe of the human spirit compelled me. How that spirit unfolds in a crisis is complex and close to my heart. The crisis I write about is twofold: the aging and death of our parents, and how these events affect us. Indeed, implicit in their aging and mortality is our own aging and mortality.

At midlife, we are at a crucial crossroads, with paths pointing us in different directions. Crowding our road is a thicket of tangled emotions. Who am I at this age? What is my existence? Who have I been at various ages? Who will I be as I grow older? These questions abound at this prickly time. We have choices to make. Succumbing to the anxieties, maybe even fears, of aging is easy enough. Dread of death and the unknown dovetail with the aging process. While it takes considerable effort, a journey of self-exploration can be far more exciting and rewarding.

When searching your self, past and present experiences are apt to pop up. Human experience is multifaceted, constructed from memories, perceptions, imagination, our wiring, our culture, and our myths.[1]* And that is some of what this book is about. Uppermost in my mind is that human experience is a dialogue between the forces of the personal and the interpersonal. So a thrust of this book is examining your self, and your self in relationships with your parents and with other people. Understanding provides you with tools to mold meaningful forms of living and loving from inchoate clay.

The inspiration of the book sprung from the aging and death of my parents and how the experience was a pivotal one for me. In exploring

*Notes for all chapters will be found beginning on page 153. See an explanation of citation style there.

my prior and current existence, I embarked on a quest for purpose for my remaining years. This could be a turning point for you, a time of self-transformation, of recreating your world, of embracing your age, as it was for me.

Another source that reinforced my ideas is my work as a psychologist/psychoanalyst. In my practice, I have been privileged to observe and participate in the personal lives of people in midlife. They are either in the process of caring for aging parents, have done so already, or will in the future. Research has further enlightened me. To my surprise, while grief and mourning is a major theme in psychoanalysis, there is a dearth of research on the process of terminal illness for the caregiver.[2]

I draw on personal experience, research, and other sources, but most important, the lives of my patients. Their confidentiality is essential; hence, I have disguised their identities and formed composites of various patients. To illustrate psychoanalytic themes with case stories, I have blended diverse interactions between patients and myself.

In the bird's eye case stories, I present some of the psychoanalytic process in which I am immersed. You read correctly! I wrote that I was immersed in the process. We psychoanalysts have been demystified. Omniscient, silent sphinxes are now curious, vocal, real people. We have shed the opaque, mute stance of traditional psychoanalysis for a transparent, lively relational interaction. Not only is the patient's inner world explored, so is the psychoanalyst's.[1]

Patients cast us in roles based on real and internal presences. Unwittingly, they induce us to enter into their familiar dramas. The air is charged with strong feelings. The confluence of patients' feelings toward us (transference) and our feelings toward them (countertransference) guide the process. Prior interactions tinge the here-and-now enactments. Together, we engage in lively, often heated, dialogue to pave the way for insight and change.

The book is also about grief, misery, mourning, and deep sorrow. If this topic seems like a downer, it is; however, there is an upside. Despair is the underbelly of hope, as destruction is of resurrection and death is of life. Imagine a life of rich, creative, and fulfilling experience. It takes dark nights of the soul to arrive at more spirited, brighter days. You have a finite time to forge a satisfying life with meaning. Every moment is precious, so go for it!

My Story

To be awake is to be alive.

Henry David Thoreau

The phone rang as I was picking up after my adolescent son. It was 6:30 AM. Who could be calling at this hour in the morning? Concern turned to alarm when I heard my sister sobbing on the other end of the phone.

"What's wrong Dorothy? Are you all right?" I mustered.

"It's not me. It's mummy. Her cancer's back; it's spread," she cried. "She's very sick."

The sinking feeling in my stomach is as vivid today as it was fifteen years ago. Was this the beginning of her end? How could I be there for my mother and my sister? We lived in different cities. They lived in Montreal and I lived on Long Island in New York. As a single working mother, I was my son's sole financial and emotional support.

I was thrown for a loop. Not by the practical logistics of this new crisis, but by my tumultuous emotional state. My son was an adolescent in transition. I too was in transition, adjusting to a new career path and my forthcoming marriage. Dizzily, I careened from crisis to crisis. No compass, no directions, no preparation for the storm of emotions. I was at sea without a rudder.

My father died three years earlier and my mother was facing death. I was next in line. My parents' mortality triggered anxieties about my own mortality. Time was short and I had much to accomplish. I had many questions and self-doubts. Would I arrive at some resolve about the conflicted relationship with my mother before she died? Would her pain be alleviated? Would she die with some peace of mind? Would I find the strength to guide my son with firmness and love? Would I be an understanding, loving partner to my future husband? Would I make it in my new career trajectory? I pondered my past experiences and wrestled with how I could use them to improve the present and pave the way for the future.

I survived. How? I got help. My son, my future husband, and my friends were my rudder. They supported me. My therapist, a psychoanalyst, was my compass. She enlightened me, helped me to accept and own my unwanted feelings, to work through old unresolved issues that surfaced, and to care for myself. I felt understood, validated, and more at peace. I began to examine my self and my relationships. The process inspired me to explore not only my existence but also the meaning of the rest of my life. In doing so, I found surprising prospects for development that continue to this day. One of the more recent opportunities was to write this book.

In my practice as a psychologist/psychoanalyst, I work with other adults in midlife. Inevitably, they are coping with the challenge of their aging parents. They feel unprepared for the chaotic emotions that affect them and their families. To help them, I draw on my clinical, research, and personal experience.

In this book, I hope you will get as much help as my patients and I have so that you may feel understood, validated, and more at ease with your emotions. In the process, I hope you will learn more about your self, your parents, and others in your life. I survived the storm and grew stronger, as do my patients. My wish is that you will, too.

Getting Your House
in Order

Change is the constant, the signal for rebirth,
the egg of the phoenix.
Christina Baldwin

What about you? Has your life come to a standstill? Feeling emotionally
in turmoil? Exhausted and overwhelmed? Fear you are falling apart?
Before you can cope with your aging parents, you must first sort
yourself out. So, getting your house in order is the first order of business.

There is good news and bad news. The bad news is—well, you know
that—your elderly parents are failing. Whether or not they are driving
you crazy, it is still an overwhelming experience. As if that is not
enough, you are dealing with changes and limitations of your own. It
may not be the best of times, but it does not have to be the worst of
times. You may feel that this is not the ideal time for personal growth.
Many of my patients and I have found otherwise. Indeed, this difficult
phase turned out to be the quintessential time for inner development
and change. Maybe the bad news is not so bad after all. Hang on.

The good news is that help is on the way; not only that—you are not
alone. A groundswell of Americans, known as the baby boomers, born
right after World War II are currently in midlife transitional stages.
Their elderly parents are living longer than ever before and need help
with activities of daily living (eating, bathing, dressing, getting in and
out of bed, toileting). In at least one third of cases, midlife children
provide this type of help.[1] Many of my patients are midlife children
caught up in a crash of developmental transitions—that of their elderly
parents coupled with their own. Although the stories or details differ,
the human dilemma is the same.

Distress is universal; so is hope. We all want peace of mind. Think about your predicament; allow your feelings to surface. Then, let me help you through this arduous time in your life. You are currently passing through a thorny, dimly lit tunnel. This spiky bypass can serve to illuminate the journey ahead for a smoother, more enlightened experience.

COPING WITH MIDLIFE CHANGES

> Time is a dressmaker specializing in alterations.
> Faith Baldwin

Your Changes

Part of what makes this phase of your journey so complex is your own aging process. Signs of aging stealthily encroach; fears swirl around and settle in your psyche. The decline of parents heightens anxiety about your aging.

You may have forgotten the name of the movie you saw last week. No big deal—or is it? Parents suffering from dementia raise a bright red fearsome flag. Is this a forecast of your future? Not really, not rationally, but fears are fears; they are not rational. And so it is with physical symptoms. Before you can cope with your aging parents, you must first explore your self and come to grips with your midlife changes.

As you begin to examine your self, you find various physical and psychological changes. Sun damage, environmental impurities, stress, mental anguish, and hormonal changes impact on your health and appearance. That is because free radicals may invade cells in your body and cause damage. Damage shows up as wrinkles or more serious degenerative disease such as heart disease, arthritis, diabetes, dementia, and cancer. Fortunately, in addition to medical treatments, we now have antioxidants and other health food supplements to protect our cells.[2] That is only one part of the secret to successful aging. Your frame of mind and a healthy lifestyle are other parts. You probably know what I am talking about: a positive outlook, exercise, a sensible balanced diet, productive work, and satisfying relationships.

Hormonal changes coupled with psychological issues are related to emotional chaos. Sleep problems often arise, either in falling asleep or in staying asleep. Many of my patients are wide awake at 3:00 AM, raiding the refrigerator. Of course, those are the overweight people. Other people sleep too much and feel tired during the day. If you are an overeater or an oversleeper, you might consider seeking professional help. Psychotherapy for psychological problems, once stigmatized, is now part of mainstream culture. Even Tony Soprano has a therapist!

Alterations in physiology may affect sexual functioning. Menopause brings hormonal changes, and some women experience discomfort during intercourse. The vaginal walls get thinner and secretion of fluids diminishes. Women may avoid sex. Avoidance only worsens the problem and is the first step to decline in the quality of intimate relationships. Over-the-counter lubricants may help solve the problem. Lots of tofu in your diet and health food supplements for menopausal women may be helpful. Recent research has shown serious side effects from hormonal replacement therapy use. Hence, I suggest that you exercise caution. Do your research first. The Internet is a valuable resource, with links to published accurate studies. A consultation with your gynecologist will yield more data that is specific to your needs.

Many men experience changes in their erectile functioning. Sorry, guys, it does not get bigger faster. But is that really what counts? If you are avoiding sexual activities because of shame, you are sure to lose out. Indeed, as the saying goes, if you do not use it you lose it. I encourage my male patients to speak to their partners about their concerns, rather than avoid them. Express some ways that your partner can help you become aroused and stay aroused. She will feel closer to you and that is what intimacy is about. Indeed, intimacy is much more than an erect penis. If you have led an active sex life till now, chances are good that you will continue to do so. Viagra is the new kid on the block, which may or may not be for you. The Internet and your urologist can inform you of its benefits and drawbacks. Everyone is different, but inevitably, we grow older. It all sounds neat and tidy, but what you are dealing with is quite messy and tangled, as seen in the following case study.

Sex on the Side

After twenty-eight years of marital ups and downs, Arlene and Phil decided they needed help. In the past, they were somehow able to fight, make up, and remain hopeful about a brighter tomorrow. This time things were different. Arlene discovered that Phil was having an affair. She was devastated. He was contrite.

Initially Phil denied the affair; however, Arlene's evidence was incontrovertible. She found another women's panties in his brief case with a note that read "the closest thing to the real thing." It was signed "Until tonight, your sugar baby, Barbie." Phil begged Arlene's forgiveness, but she was inconsolable.

"Would you believe it? Why now? It's bad enough he cheated on me with that tramp. What's even worse—if there could be a worse—is his timing. My mother has pancreatic cancer and she's dying. I feel like I'm dying also. I need Phil's support now more than ever. So, where is he? Happily humping that twenty-three-year-old slut, while I'm changing bedpans. Our daughter is only two years younger than his whore. His apologies mean nothing. He's full of shit." Arlene spewed out her scathing words.

Arlene yelped like a wounded animal, then broke down and wept. Her rasping sobs reached over to me and landed with a thud. Phil felt the impact of her pain. Face down, looking dejected, Phil handed Arlene a tissue. Throwing the entire box of tissues at him, Arlene hurled more insults. Pleadingly, Phil turned to me.

"Now you can see what I'm going through. This is good; you should hear what she says at home. I know I did the wrong thing, but she's such a bitch. She never wants sex. She gives herself to everybody except me. Her mother, the children, and her job all come first. I come last. When she finally agrees to have sex, I can't get it up." Phil was getting worked up now.

"Why do you think that is?" I asked.

"I don't feel like a man with her." Phil exclaimed.

Arlene had kept her cool until now, but this was too much.

"But you can get it up with Barbie, that slut?" she shouted. "You're pathetic, you're a loser. You can't even accept responsibility for what you did. You're no good. I'll bet you're screwing your patients. Which cavities are you filling, Philly?" Phil was proud of his orthodontist practice, so Arlene's sarcastic wit hit a sensitive nerve.

Arlene, a blue-eyed, curly blond woman revealed two endearing dimples when she smiled. Lately, she was not smiling much. She was bright and caustic, but there was another side to her. Arlene was also kind, considerate, and loving. It seems her menopausal changes had affected her emotionally. She felt more edgy, irritable, and sensitive. Phil's behavior was more than she could bear.

She explained that she did not mean to reject Phil, but sex was painful for her. She had trouble sleeping and was up most nights worrying about her mother. So she was not up to sex as much as she used to be. She said she tried to get Phil aroused, but he did not respond. His impotence left her feeling undesirable.

Phil had a boyish look, despite his salt and pepper hair. His navy blazer was casually open, sporting a cotton knit shirt and khaki pants. He could be articulate and charming. He could also be maddening.

Phil's side of the situation was that he, too, had undergone changes, maybe not menopause, but still changes. He did not like where the extra twenty pounds settled—around his middle. He felt ashamed of his body. Not only was he slowing down physically, his back hurt, and he noticed some memory lapses. Arlene was not supportive of him. Phil felt insignificant with her; most important, he felt impotent with Arlene. Barbie, on the other hand, was attentive and sexy. He was everything to Barbie; with her, he felt potent and young again.

Exploration of Arlene's early childhood uncovered experiences replete with disapproval and abandonment by her mother, who constantly corrected Arlene's fast speech, unruly curly hair, and short skirts. Arlene responded by rage attacks on her mother, which she later repeated with her husband. Her mother punished her by retiring to her bedroom, blaming Arlene for her high blood pressure that was certain to kill her. Her father, a hard-working man, was rarely home; when he was home, he refused to get involved with the mother-child disputes. Unable to cope with Arlene's behavior, her mother sent her off to a private girls school. True to form, her father did not intervene on Arlene's behalf, leaving her feeling rejected by her mother, betrayed by her father, and abandoned by both. Given her past experiences, Phil's betrayal of her was unbearable. Now that her mother was dying, the old abandonment and guilt issues were revived, as were fears of aging. Phil's betrayal of Arlene with a younger woman was yet another cruel insult.

In therapy, Arlene got in touch with her hunger for approval and the way she sacrificed her self for others to gain that approval, particularly her disapproving mother. Soon she could see how her insatiable needs and fears pushed Phil away rather than drawing him closer. When Phil did not respond quickly or sensitively enough, she became demanding and critical, only incurring further distancing by Phil. The extramarital affair was the final distancing act that brought them into therapy.

Once Arlene saw how her childhood issues were being played out in the marriage, she and I embarked on a project of creating her sense of self as worthwhile in her own right. When Arlene married, she shelved a wonderful talent for animal photography, which she now dusted off and plunged into whenever she could find time. She realized that aging was inevitable, so why not make it a successful transition, with self-care the first order of business? She joined a yoga class, began eating healthy foods such as tofu, taking vitamins and supplements, and purchased an over-the-counter lubricant so that she could enjoy sex with Phil. The change was remarkable! With a greater focus on her self and less on Phil or others for approval, Arlene felt and projected vitality, sexiness, and excitement.

Last and most important, Arlene worked on forgiveness of her parents, her self-neglect and, of course, Phil. Her task was made easier by her newly found self-respect and by Phil's attentions. When he became aware of the deep pain he caused, he went to great lengths to make amends. Instead of finding sex and excitement with others, he decided to revive the marriage, by bringing novelty and romance into it. What's more, he now had a vital, sexy wife with whom to play.

One day, out of the blue, Phil surprised Arlene by coming home at lunchtime, grabbing her and fervently ripping off her blouse. Arlene squealed in delight, and launched into a raunchy striptease that culminated in mad, passionate lovemaking. The spontaneity and feeling of the forbidden, which he found with other women, was now an integral part of the marriage. To top it off, he encouraged Arlene's photography and secretly built her a darkroom, which was unveiled on her birthday.

What made the metamorphosis possible for Phil? Similar to Arlene, Phil had early childhood issues that resurfaced. Phil's mother died when he was four, and his encounter with love, warmth, and intimacy was cut short. He was the youngest of three boys who were raised by their strict father and attentive, but lukewarm stepmother. He did not recall any emotionally intimate relationships with women prior to Arlene. Yes, he had sex with them. When they got close to him, however, he cheated on them, only to repeat this pattern with Arlene.

In therapy, Phil relived the early central loss of his mother and his terror of intimate attachment, lest he face yet another painful abandonment. Now that middle age was upon him, Phil had choices to make: to persist in his distancing behavior of adultery or to risk a commitment of intimacy with Arlene. He could also see how he found affairs arousing; indeed, they were forbidden, novel, and most important, without a commitment, they were safe. In these liaisons, he was in control of the length and depth of the relationship, which is antithetical to a healthy intimate relationship. Also, if one does not get too close as in extramarital affairs, one wards off a possible abandonment. Hence, nothing gained, nothing lost. Phil chose to take the risk for greater gains that intimacy provides, and finally made a commitment to the marriage with his wife.

Instead of fearing his declining sex drive, Phil began to discuss his concerns and to express ways that Arlene could help. Their discussions of sexual needs acted as foreplay and sex became an arena for greater communication and intimacy. Lo and behold, lust followed. When problems arise, instead of turning away from each other, they now find it easier to turn to each other.

In the preceding case, you can see how age-related changes exacerbated personality issues. Aging was only one part of the equation; both Arlene and Phil had to resolve old issues and see how these issues played out in the marriage before they could find intimacy with each other. All in all, the process is complex, but not prohibitive.

Your Reality: How You Look at It

When I look I am seen, so I exist.

D.W. Winnicott[3]

We don't see things as they are,
we see things as we are.

Anais Nin

There are changes, but do they have to be onerous? It depends on how you look at it— on what your reality is. In current postmodern times, the whole meaning of reality is being questioned. What we refer to as reality is constructed by our participation.[4] So, if a tree fell in a deserted forest and no one ever saw it fall, did it really fall? The participation of the observer is what brings the event into reality. We understand our selves as partners in our reality.

In the Arlene and Phil story, their versions of reality differed. Before they could make changes in their relationship, they had to learn to see changes in their aging process in another light. Clarity about the past fortified how they would participate in the present relationship. Only then could they better understand themselves and relate to each other.

What areas of this book speak to you? With what areas do you resonate? How you apply yourself differs for each of you. It may even vary depending on your mood. What you bring to this book makes it live or die for you; how you participate in reading the text. By the same token, how do you want to participate in your midlife changes? How you look at it, depends on what you are about—who you are.

Your Self

And the time came when the risk to remain tight in a bud
was more painful than the risk it took to blossom.
Anais Nin

Before you can make good choices, a journey into your self comes into play. So, what is a self? I posed that question to a group of people. At first, responses were tepid; then a lively debate arose.

In Search of a Self

"A self is a soul," Olivia shyly remarked.

"It's also a body," brawny Brian quickly retorted, and everyone laughed.

"It's being a good person," Justine ventured. That one sparked interest.

"It's being real. It's not being fake," Tom piped in.

"Are you suggesting that I'm fake? Look who's talking. Your toupee's not exactly real." Justine the "good person" struck out at Tom.

"It's being a well-rounded person; it's a lot of things." Sure enough, Mike the mediator stepped in. Now we were on to something.

"What things?" I asked the group. People volunteered a lot of things.

"My feelings make me a self," whispered lovely Lindsay.

"My memories," offered Agnes, who was aging.

"When I think of my self, I think about my mind," Peter pondered the question.

"When I think about my self, I think about my family, " offered Florence.

"For me it has to do with my work. At work, I'm somebody; without my work, I'd be nobody. I wouldn't have a self," explained Emily.

" I used to think I lost my self in my art, but I realize that I find my self there," Arthur responded.

And so it went, on and on. People bounced off each other, reacted to each other, made contact and connected. A prominent subject that emerged was that a self has many parts. Another salient theme was that people were relational and social and interacted with each other.

A self is a complex mix of many parts and people. Yet, we maintain an essence—a true self. Think about a puréed vegetable soup with a number of ingredients, each one with its own distinct flavor and texture. Once blended, the ingredients cannot be separated as they have lost their distinctiveness. Yet, if you use enough tomatoes, you can discern it is a tomato soup and not an asparagus soup.

One part of the formation of who we are today is our genetic background—our inherent nature or temperament. Another component is steeped in the past, in early childhood relations. Postmodern psychoanalytic thinkers refer to people as relational selves, and find that interactions with caregivers transform the inner state with which children begin.[3,5,6,7]

An interaction implies a two-sided relationship. One part of the interaction is how our caregivers responded to aspects of our temperament. The other part is how we reacted to their responses. Our reactions were influenced by our basic nature, how we felt at that moment, and the environment. Our caregivers' responses to us and our reactions to them form the basis of interactions with other people.

As we move on with our lives, we carry this pattern of relating along with us. It may work in some cases and not in others. It may be in play when interacting with elderly parents. I would like to underscore another vital aspect of our makeup. The defining characteristic of our humanity is the ability to exercise free will, to make choices, and to create and re-create our selves. In the analogy of the vegetable soup, we are in the soup and out of it. We are both the blended self and the chef who chooses the ingredients, as seen in the following family case study.

It's All in the Family

Carol was rounded in all the right places. Full-bosomed with flaring hips, she was the epitome of maternal warmth and comfort. Tall and slim, Jim was built for efficiency. While they did not see eye to eye on many issues, they were a team. They were in accord on Gregory, their seventeen-year-old son, and Samantha, age twelve. They depicted both children with distinct temperaments from birth. Gregory was the easy, happy, contented baby; Samantha was the difficult, fussy, hard-to-comfort baby.

"Greg was a pleasure. Jim traveled a lot then, so it was just Greg and me for a while. Greg was always creative and I encouraged it. He's still artistic," Carol beamed.

"Greg was a good baby, but now he's making terrible choices. He bleached his hair, pierced his eyebrow, and hangs out with the wrong crowd," Jim complained bitterly, and went on. "Greg has no patience for anything or anyone. My sick, elderly mother lives with us. Greg's so hard on her," Jim explained.

"Why do you think he changed so much?" I asked.

"Sam was born, for one thing," Carol said pensively. "She was a colicky, demanding baby. I remember her crying all day and night."

"What do you think, Jim?" I queried.

"I think Carol catered to Greg when I was away. When Sam came along, Carol was pulled away from Greg," Jim retorted.

Carol agreed with Jim and blamed herself for Greg's conduct.

"I notice Carol takes the blame for Greg's behavior. Jim, do you think you have an influence on the children?" I turned the focus to Jim.

"Yes, I set rules in the house and I expect my kids to follow them. Now take Sam, she's no problem. I'm proud of her. Her grades in school are excellent. She dresses like a young lady and has nice, clean-cut friends. You should see how good she is to my elderly mother." Jim was pleased with himself.

"You think she's so terrific and in many ways, she is. But she has problems, too. She's obsessive about things and she's afraid of her own shadow. And not only that, Sam is a perfectionist," Carol spoke up.

So, not all went as expected. Early temperaments did not quite auger future behavior. As the dialogue continued, certain themes emerged. Sam and Greg were born with different dispositions. Carol and Jim's contrasting personalities and responses to their children had an influence. Circumstances also intervened.

Eager to be a super mom, Carol was there in spades for Greg and he thrived on it. Actually, she was ready to feed Greg even before he cried. In infancy, Greg did not have a chance to experience an optimal amount of frustration. Five years later when Sam was born, Greg fell from the pedestal. As an adolescent, he showed low frustration tolerance. So, it was Greg's nature, his mother's response, and his reaction to it that contributed to Greg's problems. Jim had a part in it too; his rules were unbending and his temper quick. When threatened, people tend to either flee or fight. Greg chose to fight. He rebelled against his father and struggled to find his own identity.

As an infant, Sam was sensitive and cranky. Carol tried hard to satisfy her and responded instantly, but Sam would howl and vomit the milk. Carol rocked Sam, sang to her, changed her, and fed her again. Sam continued to cry until she finally exhausted herself. Greg also wanted mommy, but there was just so much to go around. Sam was an anxious baby who, as a preteen, continued to be anxious.

Jim overcompensated for what he saw as Carol's overindulgence and permissiveness by setting rigid rules, enforced with severe punishment. Jim's rage reactions to her brother scared Sam. She chose to flee, hide her real self, and adopt a false self. Sam became compliant. Instead of being her true self, she conformed to please her parents. Afraid of losing favor with them, Sam was trapped in a jail of perfectionism.

You can see how complex these interactions are. For every action, there is a reaction. The blend of nature, nurture, and relationships with caregivers shapes what we call the self. Samantha and Gregory were young people in search of their true selves, as are many people their age and our age.

In family therapy, the members got in touch with their feelings and their impact on each other. Carol began to set limits and Jim reacted by loosening the reigns of control, which had a ripple effect with the children.

Embarrassed by her developing breasts, Samantha initially slouched shyly in her loose, baggy clothes. Her whispery, timid speech was childlike, as was her giggle. Jim had made great efforts to control his self rather than others; slowly Samantha summoned the courage to speak up and even speak back to her father. Jim, surprisingly, kept his cool, which met with Carol's approval. She also praised her daughter's more assertive behavior. Sam learned that she need not fear her father, nor did she have to contort herself like a pretzel to be loved. Lately she stands up straight, proud of her body, and speaks in a clear voice.

At first, Greg refused to join the family in sessions (more defiance, coupled with fear of further condemnation). Eventually he did come to a session "to see what you guys are saying behind my back." Feeling safe, he continued in therapy. Also, he admitted he felt left out and was curious to see what was going on. Greg experienced the change in his father as genuine, with a real wish to bond with him. Father and son set up a series of bonding activities—ball games, action movies, and guy time. Carol had more time with Sam, which they spent in mother-daughter feminine pursuits. When the family got together at mealtime, the atmosphere had changed—there were more loving exchanges.

Projections

If you hate a person, you hate something in him
that is part of yourself. What is not part of
ourselves does not disturb us.

Hermann Hesse

People seem not to see that their opinion of the world
is also a confession of their character.

Ralph Waldo Emerson

At this juncture of your life, you may look back and see good and bad experiences. All you have gone through bears on who you are now and how you relate to others,[8] especially your elderly parents. If they are ill, frail, cranky, demanding, or raging, caring for them is hard to bear. Rationally speaking, painful experiences enrich and deepen your personality. In a heated moment, thinking rationally is not so easy, and you may well explode. Then you hate how you have reacted. You may even think, "It's not like me. I didn't want to do it; it just came rushing out."

Understanding our selves is crucial to controlling our behavior. Knowing our selves is about the relationship we have toward not only what we love in our selves but also what we hate about our selves. We usually cherish our loving qualities and dread our hateful ones.[8] People like to see themselves in a good light, so they may create a false or ideal self of who they wish to be, not who they really are. Keeping odious characteristics out of awareness, while spotting them in others, is a method used to protect an ideal sense of one's self.

The process of disowning negative qualities and finding them in others is called projection. People avert facing their hateful characteristics by unconsciously placing them into other people. The analytic phrase is that they project them onto others. Hence, if we despise our aggressive behavior, we are sure to split it off from awareness and find it in other people.

A related unconscious process known in analytic circles is projective-identification. So, if we dread our rage, we suspect rage in others. Inevitably, our attitude comes across to them and they respond with anger. Then the anger is out in the open for us to loathe in them, instead of loathing ourselves. We have provoked the other person; they have identified with the aggressive role we have cast them in and have acted accordingly. Similarly, if we don't own our neediness and insecurities, we provoke others to behave in needy and insecure ways, as in Henry's story.

Henry's Other Half

Henry was bigger than life. A former professional wrestler, he parlayed his pugilistic skills into fighting for dollars. Trading on the stock market, he made a lot of money. There was nothing subtle about Henry. The burly body adorned with gold and diamond jewelry, the expensive, form-fitting clothing, and his flirtatious manner left little to the imagination. He thrived on attention. Henry was in individual analytic therapy with me, but the specter of his wife Marilyn was always in the room. He berated her constantly and pitied himself.

"She's self-centered and mean. She wants to consume me. I've got to tell her how beautiful she is every few seconds. She wants me to drop everything, kiss her, and profess my love to her whenever the whim strikes her. I work out of the house, but I work hard so she should have everything she wants. The big house, the Mercedes, and the private schools—it's me who pays for it, not her. She gets to enjoy it. She doesn't understand that I can't pay attention to her full time, that I have to work. It's all about her. All she does is sit on her pretty ass. Sunday I was relaxing and watching the ball game and she shut the TV off. All week I heard that I was a bastard, selfish, and cruel to her." Henry's harangue had begun.

"It sounds like Marilyn wants more of you. Is she insecure about the relationship?" I noticed that I referred to his wife as Marilyn. Henry distanced himself from his wife by calling her "she." Unconsciously I tried to bring her closer to him.

"Insecure is only the half of it. She's needy and she nags. Not like you, Doc, I'll bet you can take care of yourself." He smiled seductively.

"So you don't think I could be needy?" I was curious.

"No way, your husband's a lucky guy." He was at it.

"Flattery will get you everywhere. But, I notice we're talking about my relationship, not yours. What gives?" I asked.

"Nothing, it's just that I can't make my wife happy. I don't get it. I'm a great husband and a super provider. Everybody knows that, except her. She claims that my work is really about me, not her. She tells me that she never wanted a fancy house, car, and expensive schools." He continued to focus on her.

"Whose idea was it?" I tried to have him look at himself.

"Mine, but she's enjoying it." Henry was determined to avoid himself.

"How about you?" I persisted.

"I love big parties and I love to entertain. I have tons of friends who love me. She accuses me of needing the world to love me; that it's all about me." He was getting warm.

"So, you think it's all about her and she thinks it's all about you. And Marilyn accuses you of being cruel and you accuse her of the same. Amazing coincidence." I began to get the picture.

The picture was multifaceted, and one of the processes was projective-identification. Henry denied his detested qualities and projected them onto his wife. His behavior was provocative and Marilyn responded in kind. He accused her of being insecure and needy. Yet he threw lavish parties, lived a showy life, and flirted outrageously to garner admiration. So, he was insecure and needy, but dreaded these qualities in himself. He distanced himself from his wife by immersion in his work and his social life. Henry provoked Marilyn's insecurities and she pursued him. In this way, he averted his insecurities and she enacted them.

Getting underneath Henry's insecurities and craving for public adoration was not easy. He held tightly on to his defensive ways of protecting his fragile self-esteem. He insisted on blaming Marilyn and me for not understanding him. According to him, entertaining others was a manifestation of his goodness, with no ulterior motive.

His father was a successful music producer and their childhood home was filled with lavish celebrity-studded parties. His mother enjoyed the reflected glory of her husband and his illustrious clients, leaving lonely little Henry to find solace with a nanny.

In time, Henry could see that he grew up in his father's shadow, feeling small, inept, and lacking in confidence. When Henry realized he was trying to compensate for these troubling feelings by repeating his father's partying style, our journey of reclaiming his self had begun. He soon saw that his father was not the giant Henry perceived him to be; indeed he had shortcomings including a gambling and a drinking problem.

Henry was determined to find other ways to feel important that would help satisfy his craving for adulation. One way was to pay more attention to his wife and children. Wishing to spare them feelings of neglect that he suffered, he went about planning vacations for the family and romantic getaways with Marilyn. His family's positive feedback and love was far more satisfying than purchasing love with strangers. Indeed, you would think Marilyn was in therapy, rather than Henry. He reported her gain in self-confidence, with more loving and less suffocating demands.

We can bring out the best selves in our loved ones, or the worst selves, as Henry discovered. Similar to negative projections, we can project positive feelings. If we feel proud of our friendly manner, we will expect it in others and act warmly toward them. Sure enough, we will get pleasant responses. Aggression begets aggression and love begets love.

To improve the relationship with your self, your parents, and other people, it is paramount that you own your hateful personality traits instead of defending against them. By being aware of and understanding your unwanted behavior, you are better able to exercise free will and make changes. Your ability to make choices plays a major part in the construction of your self and your experiences.

Your Relational Self and the New Physics

> The meeting of two personalities is like the contact of two chemical
>   substances;
> if there is any reaction, both are transformed.
>   Carl Jung[10]

The term *relational self* refers to your self in relation to other people. Contemporary modern relational analysts posit a fresh, multilayered perspective. They contend that unconscious attachments are unique to each person, and are formed in the person's early childhood patterns of relating.[6,9] What is more, these attachments are transformed over time and influence interactions with others.

An earlier analytic perspective is that unconscious connections are not personal. Instead, they are universal, with a common psychic substrate. The tie to prior people is known as the *collective unconscious*. Carl Jung suggested that we are linked to archetypes or primitive images that have existed since the remotest of times.[10]

The new physics brings another fascinating dimension to the experience of our relational selves. In concert with both schools of analysis, quantum physics thinkers hold that we are all linked and we shape each other. They arrive at their position from another viewpoint based on laboratory science.

Studies in quantum physics[4,11] suggest there is a collapse of time and space. In a laboratory experiment, changes in a subatomic particle occurred spontaneously and simultaneously to another particle in a different laboratory.[4] Similar phenomena are part of the human experience. How often have you found yourself thinking about someone when they call you? How about the feeling of *déjà vu*, that something you are experiencing now has happened before? Another notable experience is our dreams. When we dream, our unconscious is at work. In our dreams, time, places, space, events, and people overlap: they are condensed and magically transformed into new images.

In quantum physics, all matter including our selves is comprised of discrete particles and undulating waves.[4] Particles and waves construct the whole and neither one can be analyzed too much in terms of distinct elements. Instead, the intrinsic nature of each element is reshaped by its relationship with other elements.[12] So, the essence of the element depends on its place within a relationship—within a context.[4]

The concepts in the new physics are akin to the pea soup analogy that I drew on earlier. I compared the puree of pea soup to your self—your essence—that is transformed by your relationships with other people.

Currently, you are in a new type of relationship with elderly parents. In this novel context, you experience your self as changing. Boundaries between you and your aging parent are fuzzy, and extricating your self from your aging parent is hard. Your emotions are over the top and you just do not feel like your self. There is also a blurring of who is who. Most important, your parents' aging process highlights and gives shape to yours.

MEDIA AND MIDLIFE

Emotionally shallow . . . dreading old age and death,
the new narcissist has lost interest in the future.
Christopher Lasch[13]

Of all the self-fulfilling prophecies in our culture,
the assumption that aging means decline and
poor health is probably the deadliest.
Marilyn Ferguson

Our culture is yet another influence that shapes the meaning of our selves. We, in turn, shape our culture, which gives rise to the notion of free will and the choices we make. The Lasch narcissistic culture is shallow, self-involved, and acquisitive.[13] The expectation of instant gratification is endemic. Unfortunately, some of the ethos that Lasch wrote about in 1979 persists today. He described the culture as "I" centered and "now" centered, with people eschewing intimacy. Superficial relationships, expectations of immediate satisfaction, glorification of youth and money were then and are now.

Television sound bites reflect the thin veneer and pseudo-insight of culture today. The media message is that in a fast-paced society there is no time for contemplation, profound thinking, or an inner life. According to the media and the mental health field, faster is better. Psychotropic medications, with possible harmful side effects, promise to replace therapeutic talk therapy. Health insurances limit talk therapy to a scant number of sessions. Caring for the welfare of patients comes last. The bottom line is profit—not for you—for the CEO.

The relentless pursuit of youth that Lasch wrote about continues to be evident. First, let us talk about ageism—the negative attitude toward older people. By the way, discrimination, a close cousin, is the unfair treatment of older people.[14,15,16] Although discrimination has been outlawed, regrettably ageism is an integral part of our landscape. Negative jokes about old age are commonplace[16] and hurtful. To add insult to injury, if you show you are offended you may get a rebuke like "what's your problem anyhow? It was only a joke." Negative songs about aging are another source of ageism.[17]

The mass media of television,[15] the Internet, movies, and DVDs promulgate not only ageism, but also sexism. Clint Eastwood and Michael Douglas play romantic leads opposite women young enough to be their daughters or granddaughters. Kathy Bates, nude in the hot tub scene of *About Schmidt*, was considered a big joke because she was over fifty and fat. Some noteworthy exceptions are the talented Vanessa Redgrave, Judi Dench, and Maggie Smith. They play roles of sage, passionate, beautiful older women, who make no pretense about their age. Meryl Streep, Susan Sarandon, and Cher are other women over fifty, who are sexy, bright, and full of vim and vigor.

Speaking of sex, vitality, and passion, when is the last time you saw a couple over sixty making love in a movie? Well, if you have not seen the independent film "Innocence," chances are you cannot remember the time. In this movie, an older couple fervently takes pleasure in a romantic, sexual relationship. Nevertheless, I have heard criticism because it showed a couple over sixty engaged in a sexual relationship. It is as though sex belonged only to the young and was off limits to folks over fifty.

Whatever happened to the idea of aging gracefully? That notion went the way of silent movies. The Internet, television, movies, and magazines bombard us with youthful images. Young, belly-buttoned singers, sexy, skinny clothes worn by anorexic thirteen-year-old models, and miracle diets are popular images. The cures for aging make it sound like getter older is a disease rather than a natural developmental stage. You cannot pick up a magazine or turn on the TV without a commercial for antiwrinkle creams or Botox hitting you in the face. For those of you who shirk exercise, tight tummies and tight buns can be yours overnight with plastic surgery. These remedies are fast, costly, and promise instant youth.

Do these superficial cultural ideals offend your sensibilities? If so, it presents you with an urgency to transcend these images and challenge the messages promulgated by the media. Fortunately, you have the ability to make choices. Now do not get me wrong. I am not opposed to makeup, cosmetic surgery, and such; it just depends on your goals. If your aim is instant youth, vitality, and romance, you will be sorely disappointed. What is more, an honest plastic surgeon will inform you that a face-lift is not a guarantee of a younger or better life. It is merely a tool; the rest is up to you. And that is not a quick fix. Coming face to face with midlife is a lengthy process, but may prove to be fruitful and transforming.

A Time of Dread or a Time of Hope

> The irony of man's condition is that the deepest need is to be free of the anxiety of death and annihilation; but, it's life itself which awakens it, and so we must shrink from being fully alive.
> Ernest Becker[18]

Death is more universal than life:
Everyone dies but not everyone lives.
                                    A. Sachs

Changes in your parents' bodies remind you of changes in your body. The close tie between parent and child exacerbates anxiety and fear that you will suffer the same fate. Your parents' pain, disfigurement, and loss of bodily and cognitive functions are harbingers of what you fear is in store for you. Their feelings of helplessness, indignation, or despair resonate with your feelings. And their vulnerability intensifies anxiety about your own.

Whether or not you follow in their footsteps is up for debate. I would argue that in today's climate, there is a good possibility that you may enjoy successful aging, better health, and a longer life. Increasingly new medications, therapies, medical breakthroughs, and healthy lifestyles have prolonged the lives of middle-aged people. Longevity has increased, and the aging process has slowed down.[19] You may become informed and avail yourself of these offerings, or you may choose to ignore them. There is one life event, however, where we have no choice. We all die.

In my practice, many people experience existential angst, which is out of their awareness. Inevitably, when anxieties and fears are not owned, they are misplaced, disguised, and cause even more suffering. Some people who do not deal with their fears turn inward and shut themselves off from others. They feel alienated and depressed. So, escape does not work. Anxious people who fear living freely constrict their existence. And so, that is not a viable option either. Danielle is an example of just this problem.

Damsel in Distress

A soft-spoken, intelligent woman, Danielle looked great in long, flowing skirts or trim shorts. Her visage was smooth, her hair was perfectly coifed, and her body was in super shape. She reported that she loved her husband, the marriage was OK, and financially they were doing fine. On the surface, all was well; however, trouble lurked just below. Danielle was obsessed with exercise, diet, grooming, and cleanliness. Actually, she was more than obsessed; these obsessions now compelled her. They ruled her life.

"I won't leave the house without my face on, no matter what. My workout comes next, then I clean the house. I'm a clean freak." Danielle admitted.

Upon further examination, we found that her routine was set in stone. If Danielle tried to deviate ever so slightly the result was disastrous. Her anxieties mounted to such heights, she feared she would lose her mind. Her husband complained that she was selfish, did things to please her self and that he felt alone. To compound everything, her elderly father's illness threatened to interrupt her rituals. His operation at 6:00 AM could not be rescheduled, and Danielle was torn. She felt obligated to be at the hospital, which left her no time for her morning routine.

"It sounds like you're in a pickle," I addressed her distress.

"You bet. His illness is hard on me." Danielle's eyes welled up with tears.

We explored the meaning of her elderly dad's illness, his death, and what implications it had for her. Turns out she feared aging, annihilation, and death.

"I clean because I'm afraid of germs," Danielle explained.

"What could happen if you didn't clean so much?" I inquired.

"Things would be dirty." She gave me a "you must be kidding" look.

"And?" I stumbled along.

"And I could get infected," Danielle responded.

"Good answer to a dumb question." I reflected her unspoken thoughts and continued. "You're afraid of contamination. Who isn't?" I joined her.

"I'll bet you're not afraid of contamination. At least not like me. I wash my hands constantly, at least thirty times a day." Danielle addressed me, yet I found myself tuning her out and tuning in to my own private musings. I thought to myself "I only wash them fifteen times a day. I guess that's a lot also." Suddenly, I realized that I was not with her. Perhaps that is what her husband experienced.

"What're you afraid of?" I returned to the problem at hand.

"I'd get sick and I could die," she blurted out.

"Do you often think about death?" I inquired.

"I'm terrified of death, I try not to think about it." Danielle winced.

So, there it was. Further dialogue about her beauty routine elicited similar anxieties and fears. Danielle feared getting older, ill like her father, and dying. In our continued work together, Danielle became aware that she managed her anxieties and fears with obsessive-compulsive acts. Compulsive routines and obsessive focus on her youthful appearance masked her fear of annihilation and death.

In denial of death, Danielle's existence had become a living death. Her rituals left no room for spontaneous fun. Her enslavement to them precluded a free, authentic, rich life. And the marriage was not really so hunky-dory. Her husband wanted a fun, sexy partner who cared more about him than her obsessions.

Additional exploration yielded her fear of uncertainty. Danielle needed a blueprint for life; every event was planned well in advance. Death, however, does not come in a neatly wrapped package. Her fear of the unknown was sparked by her father's illness. She was beset with questions. What would happen to her after she died? What about her children and her husband? What if her husband died first—would she be alone? Her agony was overwhelming. Danielle had a decision to make—to persist in her denial of death and exist with constrictive anxieties, or to choose living freely and spontaneously.

Danielle remembered her childhood home as messy, oftentimes filthy with dirty dishes in the sink, food-stained countertops, and empty liquor bottles strewn about. Her mother was severely depressed and drank as a pick-me-up. Danielle often returned from school to find her mother passed out cold on the floor, with the house and children neglected. Danielle, the oldest of six children, cleaned up the mess, straightened things up, and tried to help her mother. Her parents were divorced, and she relished her weekend visits with her father. He was fastidious, with Danielle fashioning her finicky behavior after her father and denouncing her mother's slovenly ways. Danielle feared if she let go one teeny bit, she might easily slide down the slippery slope to repugnant replication of her mother. Danielle's efforts to control her home, her body, and her future were now out of control. While her life was totally regimented, her spontaneity and *joie de vivre* were squelched.

When Danielle became aware of her irrational fears, and what she was missing of good living, she was able to combat them. She began taking small incremental steps of exposure to her fears. Soon, Danielle was able to tolerate a dirty dish without jumping up to clean it, laundry unfolded, a crumpled shirt, and smudged mascara (from laughing at herself). The world did not crumble into decay, she did not turn into her mother, nor did she become infected by germs and die. To the contrary, she began to live.

Summoning her courage, Danielle decided to pursue a dream she had always harbored. She went back to school to complete her college education. What happened to her anxieties and fears? Well, she still had them when she returned to school. She feared she would be older than the other students, that they would be smarter, with better memories and that she would fail. Danielle's experiences proved her anxieties unfounded. Her grades were stellar and she graduated cum laude.

Danielle took a quantum leap, tried uncharted territory, and allowed experience to teach her. The more good experience she had, the less anxious she felt and the more confidence she gained. By the way, her persistent obsessions and perfectionism, which had been her undoing, worked for her. Whereas others may have slacked off, Danielle persevered. Her fears were overshadowed by excitement about new prospects and challenges.

Some people, while denying death, enact their fears in other ways, as in the following case study.

Victor the Younger

Victor preferred to be called Vic, which he believed was younger-sounding. Vic was charming, with a great sense of humor. His clear blue eyes fringed with dark lashes were his defining feature. Windows to his soul, his sorrowful eyes were speckled with childish delight. He was fetching and, indeed, fetched numerous and sundry ladies. The common denominator of these darlings was their youth and vitality. According to his friends, Vic had it all—the stability of a marriage, with lots of fun outside of it. His wife was beautiful, his business successful, and his kids were doing well. The fly in the ointment was that Vic was miserable. He was depressed, ate and drank too much, and could not sleep or focus on anything meaningful—not his self, his work, his wife, or even his beloved children.

Vic was besieged with guilt and indecision. He was not ready to leave his marriage or to give up the young lovelies. In their company, miraculously, Vic came to life. He was vibrant, sparkling, and felt youthful. Halle, the newest flavor of the month, was like a drug to him. He craved her and organized his life around liaisons with her.

"Vic, it sounds like Halle's your drug." I teased him about his habit.

"Yeah, Halle's my heroin," Vic responded offhandedly.

"How do you spell heroine?" I went after his unconscious.

"H-e-r-o"—Vic suddenly stopped, and batted his lashes in bafflement.

"Halle's your heroin, with and without the "e". You're addicted to her so she's your heroin. She saves you from your self and then she's your heroine," I clarified the joke.

We both laughed and enjoyed the levity of the moment.

"I think I'm afraid of getting old." Vic became pensive.

"You think?" I joined him.

"Yah, I think." He was playful again.

"What else?" I asked.

"I'm afraid of dying." He was dead serious.

"Why?" I asked.

"I'm afraid of dying without ever having lived. This isn't living." Vic's eyes spoke of sadness.

"So, your existence is a mockery, not the real thing." I merged with him.

"I never had the real thing. My old man was a cruel slave master. I hated him, but I was afraid of him. I always got roped into doing what he wanted and not what I'm really about. I worked from the time I was eight and never had a childhood or adolescence. He died a horrible death, like the horrible life he lived; he shot himself." Vic was steaming.

"How violent!" I reflected.

"You'd think I'd be done with him. I'm finally free of him, but I'm not. My wife's just like my father. She's like my controlling father." He shouted.

Further discussion revealed Vic's fantasy of turning the clock back and re-creating his adolescence. In trying to form an identity that was not based on his true self, he toyed with various aspirations, goals, selves, and flimsy relationships. In his futile quest for eternal youth, Vic was denying death. As a result, he was left feeling confused, indecisive, and depressed. He had choices to make—to say, enough of this suffering, live authentically, or to keep running away from his self and his aging process.

In our work together Vic made a choice. He chose to live in more realistic, creative ways. He continued to explore his self in greater depth, and he came to see that many of these young women exploited him as his father had exploited him. Of course, he exploited them in return. He spent a lot of money on them, paid their rent, and bought them clothes and expensive jewelry. So, he purchased their love, and in that sense he pleased them as he had pleased his father. He decided he would find better ways to feel loved and complete.

Finally, Vic decided to focus on his marriage and see if he could be a better husband and father. In that way, he would transcend his self and find greater fulfillment. He took his wife on a romantic trip to the Greek islands and tried to rekindle their love. He told me it was just OK, not like it would have been with Halle, but he wanted to keep working on it.

When he spoke about his children and grandchildren, his face lit up. He not only loved them, but he guided them. Instead of finding his youth with the young lovelies, Vic recaptured it with his own children and grandchildren. His involvement was heartfelt and filled him with pride and joy. He helped his children with their education and jobs and doted on his grandchildren. Most important, he really got a kick out of it all.

In these new ways, Vic was no longer the reactor; he was the actor. In transforming his definition of his self, Vic felt more powerful and real. He was not at the mercy of others so much and was better able to take control of his self. He now awakens to sunshine rather than gloom. Not only that, Vic maintained a mischievous gleam in his eyes. As for his marriage, there are good days and bad ones. On this decision, the jury is still out.

Like Danielle and Vic, you too have choices to make. This could be a time of dread or a time of hope. You may continue to despair, reliving the past, or you may choose to recreate your self and look forward to new experience. I think the hardest thing for me to come to terms with about my parents' death was that they had not lived fully and richly. They both had sad childhoods and as adults, they missed out on life. The tragedy of life is not in dying; it is in not living well.

The first half of the ball game may be over, but you are not. You are just getting warmed up. The real test is now. How you play the remaining innings determines whether or not you win. Play to win and guess what? You may even hit a home run. It is never too late. You may begin the process of renewal, no matter what your age.

The social climate is perfect for transformation. Our world is in flux, with rapid changes, ideologies, and shifting societies.[20] Almost overnight countries have moved from dictatorships to new democracies. If you are thinking about a career change, the gods are with you. Although ageism persists, discriminating about age in the work place is now illegal.

What is winning about? It is about re-creating your life with a sense of inner worth, purpose, and meaning. The process of providing care for elderly parents, in and of itself, entails studying meaning systems and life histories.[21] Meaning is manifold and each person creates a purposeful life in his or her own unique way. You may be thinking that is well and good for another time. Currently, you have more pressing problems, as expressed by the following group members.

People Protest

Sally, a petite blonde, tearfully turned to me with, "How can I think about my self, when I'm caring for my elderly, ill parent? I'm suffering right along with her."

Then there was Lee, a well-known songwriter, whose father was dying, "I used to write happy, peppy songs; now my music's become morbid and deadly. I'm dying with him."

An objection from Ronald, an attorney, "With all due respect, Doctor, this isn't the time to talk about inner value. First things first."

Alexandra, an agitated, single working mother, cried out, "My mother's dying, I have too much to do, too much stress. I can't think of me."

Adult children often become enmeshed with their elderly parents while providing care, as seen in the vignette above. There is a loss of boundary and they do not separate themselves from their parents. Caregivers lose themselves and suffer their parents' pain as their own. Extricating themselves from the morass of feelings to focus on their own lives seems impossible. What is more, the process gives rise to the final separation—death.

As the hangman's noose draws closer, living a life with meaning is more urgent than ever. You cannot afford to deny your mortality anymore. Accepting death does not mean succumbing or giving up; that only leads to feelings of helplessness and depression. Accepting death signifies coming face to face with its reality. It means that you marshal your forces to begin the process of self-transformation.[22] When do you begin? There is no time like now.

Seize the moment! Make it count by imagining, by dreaming of how to revitalize your self. Many a goal has begun with a fantasy, a wish. I am not suggesting that you put your plan into action just yet. That will happen when the time comes. Formulating the future begins in the present—in your mind.

As for the past, use it to inform the present. That does not mean to bemoan prior mistakes. Belaboring hurtful relationships, wrong paths taken, or opportunities lost is a waste of energy. It will not help you move forward. You just get stuck. Standing up to challenge and taking risks are daunting, but are also exhilarating. Think about it.

LIMITATIONS

> If there is tragic limitation in life, there's also possibility.
> What we call maturity is some kind of balance
> into which we can fit creatively.
> Ernest Becker[18]

The limitations of midlife may be rude awakenings. Indeed, a decline in physical appearance or strength in midlife may undermine one's self-esteem. Analysts call these knocks to self-esteem "narcissistic blows."[23] When self-esteem is at stake, we go to great lengths to protect it. However, under the stress of coping with deteriorating parents, self-deceit collapses and we cannot help but acknowledge the realities of our limitations.

Paradoxically, we have incredible, creative minds, capable of symbols and wondrous possibilities; yet, we are chained to concrete, mortal bodies.[18] Symbolic selves have a certain freedom to imagine, fantasize, and create infinite new vistas here on earth and in space. Nevertheless, a finite body and a finite existence on earth imprison this same free self.[18] Hence, the duality of self and body is the basis of our strength and also our limitation.

At this phase of your life, when caring for your aging parents, your limitations light up, while your strengths fade into the background. Why not place both your possibilities and limits under the same spotlight. What do you see now? Sure you lose some, but you certainly win some. Perhaps you have backaches. But you have more backbone now. A little sagging here and there is no match for sagacity; they both come with middle age. Not feeling as vigorous as you did in earlier years? I do not know about you, but I wasted a lot of energy back then. Passions were scattered and spent recklessly. With less time, my focus now is more directed. Each moment in time is important. My passions are stronger than ever; they are just not the same.

Things are different now; we are entering an era of wisdom. As we age, we sage. The wild, wanton days of yesteryear have given way to more sober, clear thinking. Less frivolous abandon does not preclude vitality and fun. A new dawn ushers in level-headedness, prudence, and new types of pleasures.

Even if we look before we leap, we can still soar to new heights. Given the limits imposed by our midlife bodies, vast possibilities are still out there. What is needed is a mature, realistic vision. The early years of life helped us to be who we are today. Hence, we are more prepared for realizing our dreams. Past and current experiences include not only fun, but sorrow and pain. All of these experiences coalesce to arrive at deeper insight, courage, and power.

NEW OPPORTUNITIES ON HOLD

> We are such stuff as dreams are made on,
> and our little life is rounded with a sleep.
>   William Shakespeare

> Imagination is the beginning of creation.
> You imagine what you desire,
> you will what you imagine
> and at last you create what you will.
>   George Bernard Shaw

Midlife is a period of coming together, of growth and change. For some of you, children are out of the house and you have more time to yourselves. For others, you are fortunate enough to enjoy good health and there is a lot out there to see and do. This is an opportune time to explore new horizons. Your engine may be revved up and you are raring to go. A huge stumbling block, however, brings you to a screeching halt. Your parents took ill and need you. The care of frail, deteriorating, stubborn, or clinging parents do not exactly fit the plan.

So what do you do now? Forge ahead and pretend the stress does not affect you—that things have not changed so much? That is not realistic thinking, and it would be tantamount to lying to your self. The challenge is to find a balance into which you can creatively fit your dreams and your demands. While moving forward may not be viable just yet, imagining your future is. Indeed, creative living begins with imagination. Check out Bob's story.

A Bump in the Road

Life and relationships are about compromise. After thirty-one years delivering mail, Bob retired from the post office. The children were grown and on their own. Bob and his wife enjoyed the grandchildren and visited them often. But they wanted a change. Bob dreamed about moving to Mexico with his wife, where housing was inexpensive and they would have ample guest rooms for his children and grandchildren. They loved the climate, the food, and the people. Bob was bilingual and planned to work as a travel agent in Mexico.

He awoke from his dream to a nightmare. His father was just diagnosed with brain cancer. Bob's challenge was to find a way to care for his father, while not abandoning his dream.

He came up with a creative solution. He postponed his plans in order to be near his dying father. Bob felt remorse about his role in the distant relationship with his father. He thought he had been too wrapped up in himself. Now, with little time left, Bob wanted to be close to his father.

When his father was in the hospital, Bob had some time to himself. He found a part-time job as a travel agent specializing in cruises and trips to Mexico. In his spare time, he researched the possibilities for his retirement. In this way, Bob found time for his failing parent and his future plans.

Another example of compromise is Charlene's story.

What's a Girl to Do?

When I met Charlene three years ago, she had just come through a divorce. She finally decided to leave her destructive relationship. The abuse had eroded her self-esteem, despite her considerable qualities. Charlene's jovial, witty personality and winning smile took a dive. She struggled to stay afloat in a competitive field as a mature fashion model. Charlene believed her life was over. She dated men, but they were all losers. Then she met Carlos, a truly good man. He valued her and was caring, sensitive, and loving. Charlene began to see her self in a better light, and they planned to marry. The wedding was set, when her mother's breast cancer took a turn for the worse. It had metastasized to her bones and she was in a hospice.

What's a girl to do? Charlene felt too distraught to think about getting married when her mother was dying. She could not imagine a celebration when all that she could think about was her mother's death.

As it turns out, Carlos was born in a small village in South America. Similar to other cultures, his people celebrate a person's life at their funeral. So, his perspective differed from Charlene's. She decided to discuss it with her mother, who insisted that Charlene go ahead with her wedding. Charlene and Carlos did go ahead with the wedding plans, but delayed the honeymoon.

In both Bob and Charlene's cases, a compromise was reached. Things are not always so simple and agreeable. The process of resolving your dilemma is complex and distressing. For each of us, priorities vary. Your decisions depend on you, your relationships, and your circumstances. There are different options for each of us.

Whatever you choose, you are bound to have second thoughts and misgivings. I would suggest you verbalize them and express yourself to someone you trust. Whether it is a friend, family member, or therapist, find someone who can listen empathically. You need support lest you feel resentful toward your parent and act out in hostile or neglectful ways.

CAREER STAGES AND CHANGES

Increasingly, midlife people are renewing themselves, and in so doing, stages in their careers come into focus. Some people think that they have reached a plateau at their job and want to move on. They desire a new career entirely. Other people have just embarked on a new trajectory. Still others think it is time to retire. Part-time work, with more leisure time, is another alternative.

New interests, passions, and opportunities are beckoning. These inviting prospects, however, are hampered by the new crisis. How can you make career changes in the name of self-growth, when your elderly parent is fading?

Again, you have choices to make. You could delay your move and hope it will wait for you. Unfortunately, someone else may fill your slot and the opportunity would be lost. Or you may hope that another break will arise later. It is a chance you take.

For some people, finances come into play. A new job or a promotion with increased salary is a necessity. The upward move often entails longer hours, which means less time with your ailing parent. Perhaps, family could help out. Or, the increase in salary may provide funds to hire outside help.

There are other aspects to consider. Not only does a work opportunity bring much-needed money, it may enhance your self-esteem. Feeling more worthwhile eases your burden. Not only that, if you put your life on hold for your ill parent, you may feel resentful. So, making the career change has benefits and drawbacks. I urge you to consider your options and priorities carefully, so that feelings coupled with rational thought guide your choices.

Role Reversal

For a man needs only to be turned around once with his eyes shut
in this world to be lost . . . Not till we are lost . . .
do we begin to find ourselves.

Henry David Thoreau

Role reversal occurs when the middle-aged child takes on the parental role of caregiver, while the parent takes on the child's earlier dependency role. One could argue that these role changes are normal developmental transitions. While sanguine, that position fails to acknowledge the psychological upheaval of role reversals. In my practice, emotional turmoil for midlife children and for their elderly parents is not uncommon.

As children we look to our parents for emotional security, protection, and comfort. Many of us harbor the illusion that they will always be there for us. When that illusion is lost, sadness, anxiety or anger bubbles up. By the same token, our elderly parents have feelings about losses; their health and vigor are waning. They are no longer the guides and the givers—the powerful ones. Instead, ailing frail parents are dependent on their children. The roles are reversed. Impaired, elderly parents who feel shame and outrage is not a surprising phenomenon.[1] Hence, caregivers and aging parents assume new, ill-fitting roles.

WHO IS IN CONTROL?

The more endangered we feel, the more control we seek;
the more illusory are the controls we strive to maintain,
the more vitality seeps out of our lives.

Stephen A. Mitchell[2]

As the caregiver, you are in charge. But are you really? Who is running whom? As an infant, the world was your oyster. With good enough parenting,[3] when you cried you got attention from your parents. They fed, changed, or cuddled you. You fussed, they rocked you; you cried, they soothed you. In effect, you controlled your parents, and in that way, you controlled your world.[4]

As you developed, you sought control of your own bodily states and your environment. Your infirm parents, however, are unable to control physical conditions or their surroundings. Feeling endangered by their aging and illness, they try to control you. Deep down inside, they feel like small, terrorized, helpless children. They fear abandonment and death, so they cling to you.

The tables are turned. When your aging, ill parents moan, they want you to comfort them. When they suffer, they wish you would soothe them. Symbolically, you are their world. But are you? Can you step up to the plate? You sure do not feel like a big hitter, particularly when you cannot meet all their demands. They may be weak and unable to care for themselves. Or, they may fuss and fume over inconsequential things. You assume other roles in your life, and you may feel reluctant to accommodate aging parents. Then there is your sense of duty, obligation, and guilt. Indeed, your new role as a caregiver is "crazy-making," as you will see in the following story.

Ring Around the Rosie

Rosemarie, a long-stemmed, dark-eyed beauty, was wilting. Nevertheless, Rosemarie managed a modicum of energy to participate in group therapy. Throwing her hands up in despair, she commiserated with other group members.

"My ears are ringing with, 'Rosemarie, do this, do that, no, not like that.' I can't get it right for my mother. She's supposed to be aging gracefully, not going backwards clumsily. She's become a demanding, clinging, hollering three-year-old. When I don't turn on a dime, she throws a temper tantrum. She hurls things, rants and raves, and even curses at me."

"She sounds like a handful. Do you have any help?" asked Ely, an experienced group member.

"She's more than a handful—she's more like ten handfuls. Yeah, I sure need help. The trouble is, I hire nursing help and she fires them. Or they quit because she's so mean to them." The strain was visible, as Rosemarie woefully explained her predicament.

"Do you have any time out, for you, that is?" asked perky Pam.

"No, but you sure look like you do. How do you find time to exercise?" Rosemarie admired Pam.

"I'm caring for my sick father, but I make time. A brisk walk gives me more energy for him," Pam clarified.

"I used to work out daily. Now my mother gives me a workout." Rosemarie regrettably bemoaned her fate.

"I know how you feel. It's not really fair to you," Emily empathically commented.

"You're right. I've given a lot and it would seem it's my turn now. But, no—my mother's back in diapers, physically and emotionally." Rosemarie voiced her ironic existential crisis.

Rosemarie and her mother had enjoyed a close, loving, stable relationship throughout the years, so the drastic childish change in her mother's behavior rocked Rosemarie to the core. Not only did she feel unable to take charge of her mother's care, she felt unable to take charge of her own emotions. Indeed, she felt out of control and overwhelmed. To address her feelings and help her reclaim her sense of balance and self-control, I recommended she begin to take control of one simple task, then another, and another, each more difficult than the previous one, thus creating a hierarchy of self-control tasks. The goal was to feel sufficiently grounded to set firm, loving limits to her mother.

For starters, we focused on regulating Rosemarie's bodily needs. Hitherto she had relied on coffee, fast food snacks, and ice cream. Her energy peaked for brief periods of time; then she crashed, feeling depleted and fatigued. Her replacement diet consisted of high protein, vegetables, fruit, and nuts, with a smattering of fun foods. While preparation was slightly more time consuming, Rosemarie soon felt she was worth it. After all, she did prepare her mother's food, so why not her own? As a bonus, her energy was more consistent throughout the day. Then, over the hollering objections of her mother, Rosemarie found her a companion and went off to the gym. When she passed a bakery, Rosemarie brought a treat of home-baked biscotti. Her mother invited Rosemarie to share the treat, which they all enjoyed. Things were looking up. Next, Rosemarie addressed her bills, cleaned off her messy desk, and actually ignored her mother's protestations.

Feeling more pulled together, Rosemarie was able to cope with her mother's behavior. She was better able to empathize with her mother's outrage at the indignities of aging and ailing. Mostly her mother feared being alone, which Rosemarie addressed by adopting an adorable gray and white therapy kitty for her mother. Her mother's hair matched the kitty and they became a winning twosome almost immediately. They slept together, ate together, and comforted each other. Rosemarie named the kitty Angel, her mother's guardian angel while her mother faced death. Finally, knowing her mother was in good hands, Rosemarie, a single woman, accepted a date and actually enjoyed it.

Other issues that arise in caring for elderly parents are illustrated in the following group interaction.

Slipping and Sliding

"My mother's ninety-four, but she thinks she's still twenty-four. She's depressed, withdrawn, and complains that she's lonely. My dad's dead and so are all her friends. I work full time at a stressful job and I feel overburdened. Physically, my mother's in pretty good health; I don't know about me." Ruth wrung her hands.

"Can she get out?" Hal was hopeful.

"That's not the problem; it's her attitude. She's outrageous! This is what she tells me: 'How can I go to a Senior Citizen Club? They're old.' " Ruth was irate. "They're old, and she's not? I saw the people at the seniors club. My mother's one of the oldest ones there. She's like a stubborn two-year-old." Despite her wrath, Ruth maintained her sense of humor.

"Yeah, it's tough. Listen to this one. My father is in a great hospice. The staff knows their stuff; they're patient and cater to him royally. In his weakened voice, he mumbles that he's in pain. I feel so guilty when I have to leave." Lyle looked down.

"Why guilt? You said he was well taken care of." Dahlia was perplexed, but understanding.

"Why guilt? It's a good question. It's bad enough that he's fading; it's when he comes alive he becomes impossible. He lets loose and yells, 'How can you go and leave me with this stupid nurse? I'm suffering, and you don't care. All you care about is yourself. You are a selfish bastard.' That's when I feel guilty." A devoted son, Lyle recoiled from his father's invective. "He's just had his pain medication. His nurse is competent and pleasant. I know he's comfortable. He's like a cranky, clinging, dependent baby. Me, on the other hand, I'm self-sufficient, healthy, and independent. So, I feel guilty. It doesn't make sense . . ." Lyle pondered his problem.

"What sort of father was he?" asked Kelly.

"Come to think of it, he was always selfish and did his own thing. It was his way or the highway. And now he's calling me selfish? And I'm buying it." Kyle recognized the irony.

"My mother died in dignity, she never complained. She'd tell me 'go home already, I'm fine.' But watching her become debilitated was devastating anyhow. I hope when I get older, I can be stoic like her. I hope I don't become a burden to my children," Gail sobbed.

"I also think of myself when I think about my mother. Sometimes, I lose sight of who I am and who she is. I can see parts of me in my mother and I can see her in me. She's stubborn and I am, too. Now, she's worse than ever. I'm afraid I'll turn into my mother." Kelly was clearly distressed.

"I also wonder about who I am now, and what I'll be like when I get old," Fred offered.

"I think to myself, was I like my father when I was a child?" Tony questioned himself.

"It sounds like there's a collision of two developmental crises: your transitional stage of midlife and your parents' transitional stage of old age. There are changes in your selves and your relationships with your parents. You're skating on thin ice and you're slipping and sliding. You may well wonder who you are and who your parents are. Things are topsy-turvy," I summarized my observance.

I offered some suggestions. "Perhaps you might focus on your strengths to help you stand firmly on solid ground. Why not zone in on your prior accomplishments and the feelings you derived from them? That could easily carry over. Many of us are in this rocky boat and patience is tried constantly. So, self-care is of paramount importance in order that you care for your parents with compassion. Quality of life is important, not only for your parent but for you. Feeling more powerful is the bedrock for empathy with your powerless parents."

In times of transition, people question who they are, and who their parents are. Are you the child, the adolescent, the young adult, the parent to your children, and now the parent to your parent? You are a composite of all these parts, so you have multiple selves. In psychologically healthy people, there is an ability to feel a sense of unity, of being a "me" while being many selves.[4] Not everyone, however, is able to suspend a sense of unity, of a "me," to allow for a state of multiplicity. They are known as single-minded, like Ruth's stubborn elderly mother.

Rigid people fear fragmentation and obstinately hold on to their perception of themselves as whole. This trait is prevalent when elderly parents do not wish to acknowledge their age or fragility. They stubbornly hold on to the illusion that they are still young and vibrant. So they are stuck in the old "me," unable to allow for changes. Nevertheless, they believe they are in control of themselves. In turn, adult children feel they are losing control, and that their parents are in charge rather than themselves.

Another way that ill parents push buttons is by putting undue pressure on their adult children. When Lyle's father refused to accept his illness and fears of death, he disowned his selfishness and projected it onto Lyle. In doing so, his father maintained the illusion of himself as a benevolent man. In reality, his hatred was destructive to him and to the relationship with his son. Whereas his father felt free to spew venom, Lyle was enslaved by his feelings of guilt.

People like Kelly fear they will become like their parents when they get old. When examining your self, you no doubt find similarities between your personality and that of your parents. Intergenerational transmission of traits and patterns of relating explains some of the similarities. While this may present a bleak picture, there is a bright side to it. As human beings, we have evolved because we are relational and social. As such, we have the remarkable capacity to negotiate continuity and change simultaneously.

When you become aware of detested parts of you that remind you of your parents, you recoil; however, it does not mean you will behave as they have. Hence, if you have been abused, it does not follow that you will become an abuser. Many people who have been abused when young would never harm their children. They are determined to give their children better lives than they have had. You can learn from your parents' distasteful words and actions, so that you do not repeat them.

That does not mean you will not have disturbing feelings. Given a faulty relationship, old uninvited feelings resurface. And your prior interactions with your parents continue to reverberate with intense emotionality. Chances are, if you experienced your parent as the powerful enemy, the intrusive one, or the critical one, you react similarly in the present. Hence, you are replaying old dramas. You could, however, find new scripts. As a small, powerless child, you had to protect your self. You do not need to now. You cannot control your parents; the only one you can control is you. Elderly parents may have the same script, but the roles have been reversed. Power has shifted from them to you.

CHANGES IN IDENTITIES

As young children, we rely on our parents for guidance, protection, and comfort, which Gould has termed the myth of absolute security.[5] The belief that our parents are omnipotent and will always be available to us is also a fantasy. When parents become ill and weak, our old myths are relinquished. Surrendering these closely held illusions may be heartbreaking. You feel bereft.

With the loss of illusions comes loss of old identities. Whereas your parents were once the omnipotent magical caregivers, you now assume these identities. In early childhood you were dependent on your parents for sustenance, security, and caring. Now they are dependent on you to satisfy these same needs.

At heart, many of us look for a close connection or merger with a magic, powerful one. That merger was formed with your parent. This type of merger is reflected in all walks of life—the teacher and the student, the movie star and the fan, the lover and the beloved. The intimate bond is now broken. Your parents' identities have changed, and so have yours, as seen in Maxine's case.

Merger and Maxine

A curvaceous blonde bombshell, Maxine exuded confidence. She bubbled with exuberance, befriended strangers, and beguiled men and women. Conversations with Maxine were wise, witty, and warm. Maxine had been practicing law for the last twenty years and was expert in her field of negligence law. How can one woman have it all? Needless to say, she did not. Problems in her marriage had been serious for at least ten years; yet, she stayed.

"What's in it for you?" I inquired about her marriage.

"It's for the kids," Maxine responded.

"The kids? " I was not impressed.

"It looks like I'm not kidding you." Maxine winked.

"Are you kidding yourself?" I kidded back.

"Yeah. At work, I'm so realistic and at home I fool myself." There was no levity in Maxine's response.

"Home is where the heart is, so it's hard to be objective," I remarked.

"Speaking about home, my mother's living with me now. She had surgery and is recovering at my house. She was the greatest mom and I appreciate everything she's done. But I don't have the patience for her now. I just want to run away from her. I'm afraid I'm neglecting her." Maxine spoke gravely.

"What sort of relationship did you have with her growing up?" I inquired.

"Super. She was the greatest mom. She praised me and applauded all my successes. We were so close. My mom was a fantastic woman. She had a brokerage firm and was president of the local Rotary Club. Like me, she was outgoing, organized, worked hard, and succeeded," Maxine recalled.

"So you identify with these qualities of your mother." I commented.

"She was my ideal, my role model. I love her." Tears welled up in Maxine's eyes and she continued, "You should see her now. She's gone from competent to incontinent. From self-sufficient to self-involved. She was the life of the party; now she's lifeless." Maxine bemoaned the changes in her mother's identity.

"What a letdown for you," I commiserated.

"It sure is. I remember her as young and robust. Now she's old and feeble. Her mind's a little feeble, too. She had a mind like a steel trap. She keeps asking me how old she is. I have to tell her the same thing seventy-two times a day. I want to scream. I can't tolerate her." Maxine was weeping openly.

"How sad." I felt her sadness.

"It's sad all right. I cry a lot these days. What's even harder for me is that I can't stay asleep. I wake up at 3:00 AM and can't fall back to sleep," Maxine explained.

"Sounds like menopausal symptoms combined with mental anguish," I suggested.

"It's about my mother." Maxine was forthright.

"Maybe it has to do with the image you've maintained of her, which has changed so drastically. She was your goddess and you worshiped her. It's tragic to see her crash and you feel like you're crashing. She was all powerful and now you're supposed to be the powerful one," I clarified the change in identities.

"I don't feel powerful. I feel like there's a hole inside of me," Maxine quietly wept.

"That hole was filled by the close merger you had with your mother," I interpreted.

"I'm losing that closeness. It's a totally different kind of closeness, and soon that'll be gone," Maxine sobbed.

Maxine was dealing with a loss of illusions. The close merger was based on her mother as the omnipotent, magical good fairy and herself as the small, helpless, dependent little girl. Once Maxine came to terms with the changes in identity, we were able to address her self as an independent adult woman. Soon, she could see that she was emotionally dependent on her husband. Maxine decided to take her life into her hands and go for marital therapy. If that failed, she would seek a divorce.

Letting go of the myth of absolute security is fraught with anguish for adult children. Holding on to the myth, however, interferes with the quality of parent care. The myth of the parent as the powerful one is in direct conflict with the reality of the weak parent. Unable to bear their parents' fragile states, caregivers may overprotect them. Keeping parents from learning about the severity of their ills is a form of overprotection. The underlying motivation may be that it spares caregivers from seeing their parents fall apart and show weakness.

Whereas parents were lifelines to children, adult children now take on the identity of lifeline to their parents. Some adult children go to great lengths to rescue their parents. I have seen adult children try heroic measures, unsupported by science, that failed. Instead of serving as lifelines, unwittingly, they diminished the quality of life of parents. A compelling need to be parents' lifelines is related to an unconscious wish to maintain parents as lifelines for adult children.[6] It is how some adult children unconsciously hold on to the old merger.

Once the myth is relinquished, the crying need to save dying parents subsides. The time has arrived to save the self and find a new identity as a mature independent person. Indeed, parent care may be a chance to develop a true sense of self as a separate person.[7] In Maxine's story she began to pull her self together. She examined how she might save her marriage—or if need be, save her self as a single woman. Maxine was shifting her identity from child to adult self. When we shift our identities toward consolidation of our selves as adults, we become protectors of our selves—our own parents.

Becoming our own parents and letting go of outdated identities involve living as separate people, being our own individual selves. While we are independent selves, we are also interdependent, social people. When we experience our selves as more whole, relationships with parents, children, friends, and lovers are enhanced.

In childhood, our sense of self and wholeness arose from within an intimate parent-child attachment. Without that warm, secure feeling of fusion, we feel empty inside. Relinquishing the myth of all-powerful mother, Maxine felt a hole inside of her self. She had relied on the old merger to give her a sense of wholeness.

Infirm parents become separate people by virtue of the fact that they can no longer care for us. Hence, we can no longer look to our parents to provide us with a sense of completeness.

Searching hungrily for fusion with someone else as a replacement is an option, but not a good solution. Beware. Desperate people take desperate measures. Looking to our selves for a sense of completeness is a better solution. I am talking about seeing our selves as separate people—a monumental developmental goal. While it is a burden, the experience of parent care is also a wonderful opportunity for psychological growth.[7]

Ironically, an identity as a separate person from parents is belied by a continued identity with them throughout the life span. Identification with parents or other role models is partly how we developed our identities. Some of us reject identification with parents. Nevertheless, in opposition, we remain tied to the original bond. Hate binds us to the person as closely as love does.

Similar values, attitudes, functions, and personality traits give us a sense of continuity and stability. Our sense of power or powerlessness, mastery or ineptitude, active or passive behavior—our personality styles have evolved partly from a close bond with parents. Now the continuity of self is challenged. Maxine identified with her mother and followed in her footsteps in personality and achievements. There was a strong, enduring bond between her and her mother.

The mother-daughter tie is intense and awesome. In my practice, I find treating a daughter is treating her mother as well. The mother is in the room, not necessarily physically, but she has a psychical presence. Mother-daughter conflicts have consequences for how daughters feel about their bodies, self-esteem regulations, career choices, and relationships to men.[8]

I have found similar ties between father and son. Difficulties in their relationships also have consequences. Asher is a case in point.

Bonds That Bind

Although Asher was a generally easygoing man, his relationships were straining. He worked as a chef in the family business, a steak house restaurant. Despite the high-calorie, savory foods that Asher prepared, his body was surprisingly lean. I wondered how he resisted stuffing himself, or did he eat out? I later learned that Asher learned self-discipline early in life.

His father ran the show, with Asher, his sister Sarah, and his brother Ken following orders. In the kitchen, Sarah did not exactly follow orders; she gave them. She ordered the food, set the menu, and inspected the dishes that Asher cooked. When his father died, Ken took over the business. Although Asher was technically a partner, he answered to his brother and his sister. He never spoke up to them. In therapy, however, Asher felt free to vent his troubles.

"Doc, I hated my father. He was cruel and heartless," Asher angrily exclaimed.

"How did you react to him?" I asked.

"I caved in." Asher looked dejected.

"So, you complied. How do you think this relationship affected others in your life?" I broadened the scope.

"Well, I made sure I didn't do the same thing to my kids. They love me," Asher beamed.

"How about your relationship with your siblings?" I continued the inquiry.

"Come to think of it, I comply with them. They take after my father. Sarah is domineering and Ken is critical. They both push me around." Asher's head hung in shame. His eyeglasses fell to the floor and Asher just left them there.

"So, try as you may, you can't move away from him. You're repeating old behaviors with your father in the relationship with Sarah and Ken. The bond with your father persists and you're in a bind," I interpreted.

Asher was abused and exploited by his tyrannical father, and he consciously renounced a similar identity with his children. Nevertheless, he held onto the intense bond with his father by assuming the scapegoat role with his sister and brother. In therapy, I encouraged Asher to address me directly and confront me when I failed him. This was not easy for Asher, but one day I was ten minutes late, and, as expected, Asher simply shrugged it off. His body language, with clenched fists and tightened shoulders, gave him away. I confronted him about his anger.

"Doc, you are way off track," he spoke up.

"I see you can get angry at me," I remarked.

"I am not angry. You are trying to put words in my mouth," he shouted at the top of his lungs.

"Congratulations, you did it. You got angry with me and you didn't get destroyed. Nor did I," I beamed.

The incident began a new, more authentic relationship, which Asher began to use outside my office. At first, the pendulum swung too far, and he was abrasive with others, but soon he adjusted himself. He sought and found an assertive, considerate stance. His siblings respected him more and he felt greater self-respect and manliness. As for the old bond with his father, it still crops up now and then. Asher is working on keeping the old style of relating from impairing his relationships.

In both Maxine's and Asher's cases, identities were formed with same-sex parents; however, identities may also cross genders. Sons may identify with some of mother's qualities, and daughters may identify with some of father's traits, as in Gabrielle's story.

Too Good to Be True

Gabrielle hated her father; nevertheless, she maintained a career identity in the same arena. Her father was a construction worker and she was an architect; so, she bested her father. Gabrielle abhorred her father's rage and his superior, arrogant manner. Disavowing her anger, she decided to be a gentle and gracious woman. With close friends and an almost full life, she was missing a soul mate. Never having been married, she feared it may have been too late.

"Why do you think you've not married until now?" I inquired.

"I'm too good to these men. They take advantage of me and I just end up getting hurt." Gabrielle sounded convincing.

"How do they take advantage of you?" I wanted to know more.

"Bill, the last guy, lost his job and I supported him. So, for two years he lived off me. He turned down good jobs because they were beneath him. He was arrogant like my father. You won't believe this. I still don't believe it. I came home one night and he was gone. His closet was bare, with only empty hangers. I later found out he had another woman." Gabrielle's face quivered with rage, but she controlled her emotions.

"How awful," I said.

"It was terrible. I loved him and thought he was my soul mate." Gabrielle's sadness was unchecked.

"Tell me what you loved about him." I was looking for deeper insight.

"Well, he was soft, gentle and didn't like confrontations. We never fought, so I was shocked when he left." Gabrielle tried to stay calm.

"You wanted someone who didn't have a dreadful temper like your dad. Bill fit the bill. He hid his anger and behaved in a hostile manner. Whereas your father's rage was overt, Bill's was covert. You knew where your father was coming from. Not so with Bill. We call Bill's personality style passive-aggressive," I explicated.

"Yeah, I managed to hold on to my father's aggression, and now I'd like to kill Bill." She tried hard to keep her anger under wraps. Gabriella's clenched fists, however, were a dead giveaway.

In addition to Bill's betrayal, Gabrielle's father had died recently. She lost both men. Mourning her loss was exacerbated by anguish over unresolved issues with her father. When she was ready, she examined her self and her prior relationships. Eventually, she decided to let go of her identity as the good and giving girl and become authentic. Instead of finding power by taking care of men, she welcomed an equal partner. A good fight was OK, too. She got in touch with her aggression, stopped hiding it, and worked on transforming her newly found aggression to assertion.

In time, Gabrielle's identity was based on a more wholesome sense of self. She chose more forceful men, who would give and take. Gabrielle is currently working on an intimate relationship with a man. He is a kind, generous man, and they take care of each other. Things are looking up.

DECISIONS ARE YOUR DOMAIN

Once the responsibility of parents, decision making is often in the hands of adult children. Deciding on the right doctor, the best treatment, or the appropriate facility brings with it feelings of self-doubt and anxieties. Something else to consider is the issue of paternalism.

Making decisions for parents is tantamount to paternalism and may bring more harm than good. A great deal of concern has arisen recently about maximizing elderly peoples' autonomy and minimizing caregivers' exercise of paternalism.[9] One exercises paternalism when intervening in parents' decision-making process, even if they submit. In some circumstances, it is appropriate or necessary. If your parents are incoherent, mentally confused, demented, or psychotic, they cannot make rational decisions. Indeed, you may well be the person best suited to decide what is best for them.

The ability to step back and assess the situation objectively is impaired by strong emotions or attitudes toward parents. The danger lies in doing too much, too soon, in the attempt to save parents. Paternalism that is excessive or premature undermines elderly parents' autonomy. Like most interventions, it all depends on the circumstances. I would suggest that you take a moment out to get in touch with your feelings. Then, in a more rational, clear-thinking state weigh all aspects before intervening.

ABUSIVE PARENTS

Role reversal is especially difficult when parents are abusive. Not so long ago, the focus of studies was the abuse of elderly patients by their caregivers. More recently, researchers have examined the abuse problem from a reverse stance—the abuse of adult children by their elderly parents. In one study of 120 adult female caregivers, researchers revealed a significant problem of abuse by their elderly parents.[10] The variable that best predicted mothers' abuse of their daughters was past and present conflict.

Adult children caring for elderly parents who report abusive behavior by parents usually reveal a long history of discord. Often, problems in parent-child relationships first become apparent during adolescence and, at times, date back to early childhood. According to still other adult children, not all abusive elderly parents have been abusive in the past. For some, the drastic change of heart is incomprehensible.

Whether parents shout, insult, curse, throw things, or spit at their caring adult children, these attacks penetrate deeply. The silent treatment is equally punitive and piercing. A great many rage reactions are exaggerated repetitions of prior high-conflict interactions. Underlying is the concept of unconscious process of projective-identification,[11] which I described earlier. When angry parents project their shame and rage onto their caring adult children, they swallow the assaults and identify with the shameful and bad parent. A fight-or-flight response follows. Hence, adult children who are abused either strike back or distance themselves. Kelly's case illustrates this problem.

Too Hot to Handle

Kelly, a redheaded, hotheaded woman, was caring for her abusive father. He fumed, fussed, spit out diatribes, and cursed at her.

"I try to keep my cool, but last night I lost it." Kelly's face was flushed.

"What happened?" I asked.

"I brought him dinner. Dad's a meat-and-potato man, and I made his favorite Irish stew. He can't digest food too well, and so I have to mash his food. I served it up in a lovely bone china bowl," she continued.

"You're one devoted daughter. You dedicate yourself to his well-being and to lifting up his spirits," I remarked.

"The trouble is he's dedicated to something else. He just wants to put me down. He's too weak to chew his food, but he's not to weak to chew me out. This is what he says to me: 'What's with the mashed food? You treat me like a baby with baby food. You're a witch.' " Kelly was getting hot under the collar.

"How terrible," I reflected.

"That's only the half of it. He grabbed the tray of food, cursed, and threw it at me. Hot mashed vegetables, meat and sauce all over my dress, my stockings, and shoes," Kelly wailed. Her face now matched her red hair.

"Wow!" I exclaimed.

"I cursed right back at him, actually threw some food back at him and left. 'Let the maid clean him up,' I thought. I've had it." Despite her fiery speech, Kelly looked abashed.

"Along with your ire, I see mortification." I aired my observation.

"He demoralized me. Would you believe a food fight? I acted like a little child. I feel ashamed of myself. But I was so angry." Kelly was, indeed, so angry.

"What sort of child were you?" I was curious about her childhood.

" I threw temper tantrums with mom, who turned to Dad to punish me. Dad made me pull my panties down and spanked my bare bottom. I refused to cry just to spite him. I was too stubborn; instead I yelled bad words and ran away," she recalled.

"So, he shamed you as a little girl and now as a big girl. You were feisty then and you're feisty now." I made connections.

"I don't feel so feisty, not good feisty anyway—bad feisty. More like the wicked witch from the west," she responded.

Kelly's father was enraged at the humiliation brought about by his illness; he could no longer digest whole food. He projected his shame and rage onto Kelly and called her a witch. In turn, she took on the identity of a young child, whose bad behavior elicited shame and rage. She acted like the witch her dad had projected onto her. So Kelly and her dad repeated old forms of interacting.

Growing up, Kelly's father, a massive giant of a man, was the dominant one in the family. Her mother, a delicate, genteel southern belle, spoke softly, politely, and adored her man. She did not believe women should be ambitious and work too hard. Instead, ladies played music, crocheted, and got involved in the arts. Kelly, a tomboy, rejected her mother's influence and identified with her strong-minded, athletic, but stubborn father. Her mother frowned on Kelly's passion for baseball, field hockey, and basketball. Sports brought Kelly closer to her father, who never missed a game she played. Kelly was clearly her father's favorite, despite the spankings, whereas her girly sister Kate was her mother's favorite child.

Bittersweet memories of her early childhood contrasted sharply with the drastic deterioration of her father. Recalling his powerful body and keen mind, so disparate with his frailty and rage, brought angry tears. Access to these feelings helped her gain insight into his plight. Empathy followed. And she could feel his rage at his decline. Indeed, she felt angry for him and for her loss of the wonderful illusion she held of her resplendent father.

Feeling shame for her role in the enactment of old dramas with her father, Kelly viewed changing her script as a welcome option. Gaining insight into her father's and her feelings was key to change. Kelly began to understand that his rage was displaced from his shame to her. It was not because he did not love her, but simply that he hated his weakened state.

Then, Kelly embarked on ways to help her father's insulted self-esteem. She engaged a retired barber who was her father's age. He came to the house, lathered her father, shaved him, and shot the breeze about the old days of sports and "stuff." She disarmed her father by joining him when he began his invective (it had lost its steam by now). Kelly expressed her outrage about the soft food, squeaky wheelchair, and loud music. What's more, Kelly always enjoyed watching sports on television. So many a night found them side by side, reminiscent of earlier times, enjoying the World Series.

Kelly's father was feisty; however, not all parents are feisty. Some are too feeble to complain; nevertheless, they may have issues about their debilitating states. Rage or withdrawal by elderly, failing parents is related to a variety of factors, but I have found a common denominator. Deterioration of body or mind impacts on self-esteem; such was the case with Kelly's father. The blow is softened if you help your aging, infirm parents to maintain their self-esteem. Attention to their grooming facilitates this aim. Makeup, shaving, hair styling, wigs for hair loss, or a change of clothes boosts self-esteem and mood.

Creating a mutual activity, as Kelly did with her father, gives weak, dependent parents a sense of autonomy and relatedness. Here are some ideas that my patients have employed. One adult caregiver, whose mother was too enfeebled to apply makeup, held up the mirror for her mother's directions. She even got her cranky mother to approve of her daughter's makeup skills. Another adult caregiver gave her mother four choices of lipstick shades. She smiled as she recognized a favorite lipstick she wore as a young woman. The mutual endeavor brought greater feelings of respect and worthiness for aging parents and caregivers. Use your imagination to create your own joint venture.

RELATIONSHIP STRESSES AND STRAINS

Frayed relationships are a fallout of role reversals. In one comprehensive study, more than half the adult children felt stresses and personal strains.[1] Indicators of personal strain were being physically worn out, emotionally exhausted, stressed in the marriage, and feeling tied down. Their personal strain was related to negative feelings that included impatience, frustration, helplessness, irritation, boredom, and guilt. In my practice, many of the adult children caring for elderly parents experience similar stresses and strains. Do some parts of this study speak to you?

Are you less tolerant with others? You may feel more like a petulant child than a mature adult. How about the mess your adolescent children leave? Jeans, jackets, and jock straps are strewn all over. They are in the midst of sorting their lives out – not their clothes. Straining at the seams, you scream out. Who is the stressed-out child now?

How about intimate relationships with lovers? Fighting more and loving less? Sufficient inner resources are in short supply, so you demand more from romantic or marital partners. You feel like a small child, yearning for a bountiful breast. Unfortunately, your partner's capacity to nurture is limited.

A healthy relationship, like a strong tree, is flexible and has the capacity to bend either way. When the stress and burden are too heavy on one side, that side falls over. That is not to say that leaning on a loved one is not in order—it surely is. It is about how heavily you lean. Getting needs met from a single source is backbreaking for your partner. The stress pushes the relationship to its limits, as seen in Yves' case.

The French Connection

Yves, a dashing, dapper man, was in a close relationship with Donna. A widower of five years, Yves was experiencing yet another impending death—that of his beloved mother. Although he had been raised in America since age six, Yves continued to sport a sexy French accent. He maintained a close relationship not only with his French mother but also with his culture. He introduced Donna to French food, wine, and love. He was her man. She was not his only woman.

"What she doesn't know doesn't hurt her," Yves justified the inequity in the relationship.

"C'est la vie." I found myself joining him.

"It's good to laugh for a change. I hurt so much." He chuckled through his tears and continued. "The only other woman these days is mamma." Yves' body caved in and he looked dejected.

"You look like a small lost child," I reflected.

"I feel lost. I lost my wife and now I'm losing my mamma. I cry to Donna a lot and cling to her. I want all her attention; her world should stop for me. It's not like me. I'm afraid I'll lose Donna also." Yves moaned in pain.

"What makes you think you'll lose Donna?" I asked.

"She fell in love with my macho image. Now I'm mush. She told me she can't stand it, that I'm suffocating her. Donna's a generous, giving woman, but she can't satisfy me. She tells me that I want her to be my mother. She could be right." Yves showed insight.

Yves' role as a debonair, strong man was reversed. Instead of Donna looking up to him, he looked to her to fulfill his insatiable needs. In therapy, he learned that he wished Donna to be his Madonna, to rebirth him—to coddle, coo, and never leave him. What he feared, mainly, was his own aging and death that his dying mother elicited.

An only child, Yves' parents were estranged when Yves was eight and he rarely saw his father. Yves remembered him as a handsome, well-dressed man with gorgeous women on his arm. Indeed, like father, like son, Yves too loved to show off gorgeous women. His father moved to Italy, after which Yves lost touch with him. The loss was agonizing and still brought tears to Yves' eyes.

His mother, a sharp and successful businesswoman, adored Yves and they had a close, loving relationship. She had a few men friends, but as to her favorite man, there was no contest. To the end, it was always Yves. Hence, the thought of losing his dear mamma so soon after his wife's death was terrifying. And he clung to Donna for dear life, expecting her to replace his father, mother, and wife.

In therapy Yves became aware of his dynamics, and how the past was being played out in the relationship. He was, then, able to see how heavily he was leaning on Donna. Letting go of the macho image, painful as it was, allowed him to explain his underlying hurts to Donna. She was sympathetic to his losses and needs, which helped Yves pull himself together more. He also sought succor with others, friends and co-workers, who were caring for aging parents. So Donna's burden was lessened and their relationship improved. He doesn't demand all of her attention, as he has other like-minded supportive people with whom he relates. You may well wonder if he inadvertently met an attractive woman in his new milieu? Well, that's another story to be continued at another time.

Diverse Role Demands

When you are going through Hell, keep going.
                                        Winston Churchill

There is no moratorium on family crises for midlife children coping with elderly parents. Often, middle-generation children juggle demands from diverse roles in the family and the workplace. Adolescent and young adult children may be struggling to separate from their parents; spouses may be in midlife crisis, whereas marriages or relationships may be faltering. Work stresses require calm, rational thinking. The additional strain of coping with infirm elderly parents more than rocks the boat. You feel you are going through hell.

The noteworthy Abel diary is a personal, documented account of Emily in the nineteenth century.[1] The biography describes the poignant struggle of Emily to provide care for her elderly father, while trying to negotiate diverse role demands. The tensions with her sibling and her estranged husband and the exhausting demands of her ailing father finally led to her demise.

Two centuries later, I work with people whose stories resemble Emily's. The distinction is that today people are informed and reach out for help, so their stories have far different endings. Let us take a peek at the group members' plight that follows.

Hell's a Place Called Home

Adele, a water-colorist, was exploring her inner landscape. Her flowing painting style bore resemblance to her fluid personal style. She was sinuous, lithe, and graceful, as were the nudes in her paintings. In both spheres, Adele's raw emotions and passions surfaced from within her depths and flowed freely. Long limbed, wearing a flattering ankle-length skirt with a sherbet-colored, gauzy blouse, Adele looked cool and collected. The folds in her skirt kept the beat of her incessantly tapping foot. Try as she may, Adele was anything but cool and collected.

"She wants me at her beck and call, so she can abuse me. After she spits out her venom she accuses me of not loving her. That's when I lose it, yell back at her, and end up feeling ugly. My paintings depict beauty, but with my mother, the scene's grotesque." Adele spoke to the group members.

"You could've fooled me. You look so lovely and composed." Sidney had a crush on Adele.

"Are you flirting with me?" Adele noticed.

"I'm admiring you. I was so upset today that I forgot to shave." Was Sidney still flirting?

"You look fine to me, Sidney." Adele flirted back, and Sidney smiled.

"Thank you kind lady." Sidney was playing.

"I guess you're distracting me. I like it, but I have to get this off my chest. My mother's driving me bananas. It's not like she doesn't have other help. It's me she wants. When I hint that I have another life, she calls me a selfish, ungrateful, worthless, bad daughter. I feel so guilty, but I have other responsibilities. I'm torn." Adele began to perspire.

"I can imagine how you feel, even though things are different for me. My mother doesn't make demands on me, just the opposite. She tells me to 'go home already.' She's stoic and tries not to show her pain, but I know it's there. I see her fading away, so I'm devastated. I'm also troubled about my thirty-two-year-old son, who's struggling with his career, and I have to help him. I see layoffs all around me at work and I'm scared I'll lose my job. My wife's in menopause and has hot flashes. She's moody and I need time for her. All in all, I'm going through hell." Jason empathized with Adele.

"I'm dealing with hormonal changes like your wife," Adele responded.

"My blood pressure's sky high and my cholesterol just shot up. The stress of my adolescent girl—her therapist told me she's trying to separate from me. I'm trying to separate from my cranky, stubborn father." Stella spoke about the stress induced by her divergent demands.

"My husband is a businessman, going through his midlife crisis. He needs me. My grandchildren need me. My adult children aren't so adult, and they need me. There's only one of me. Lately, I feel like I'm going to explode." Adele wrapped her arms around her chest. Her fresh gauzy blouse was drenched in perspiration. The hue changed from sherbet to scarlet.

"It sounds like you're all going through your own private hells at home. It takes valor to hang in and to negotiate diverse role demands and developmental stages of your families." I summarized the group members' problems.

Despite various issues, in finding commonalities with others, group members felt connected and comforted. You may recognize parts of your self in these examples, and you, too, may find solace in knowing you are not alone with these issues. Connecting with others in dealing with mind splitting diverse role demands provides a respite, and what's more, it feels good.

Out of the depths of despair, in the company of other supportive people, hope may well surface. Trying on new self-enhancing behaviors with others is helpful. When all looks dark, their positive feedback brightens things. Indeed, a new way of looking at the same thing, which only another person can offer, opens the door to feeling stronger. Courage is also contagious.

ADOLESCENTS IN DISARRAY

> One is not born a woman, one becomes one.
> Simone de Beauvoir

Historically, the adolescent identity crisis has been stormy. Some describe it as a smooth, normal transition. I have found that, more often than not, the transition from childhood to adulthood is anything but smooth; it is tumultuous. Adolescence marks the transition from childhood to adulthood. One foot in childhood and one foot in adulthood, adolescents have clashing wishes. Fantasies of staying attached, coddled, and taken care of conflict with the wish to be a separate individual—a person in one's own right.

In early childhood, the influence of parents held sway. In adolescence, peer culture holds sway. Emulating popular images or celebrities, adolescents try to form their identities as separate people. They wish to express their individuality and their emancipation from parents.

A separate individual entails making good choices. In our current climate, taking the right road is more difficult than ever. Getting lost in drugs or alcohol has dire consequences. Promiscuous, unsafe sex is equally perilous. Adolescent depression, anorexia, bulimia, self-mutilation, and suicide are alarming states. Although they reject help, adolescent children need parents' guidance more than ever.

It is not uncommon for adolescents to express rage at their parents, rebel, and engage in defiant and dangerous behavior. Ironically, in adolsecents' efforts to be separate people, their risky behaviors keep parents glued to them. Finding telltale signs of dangerous activity, parents begin to snoop on them. In my practice, I meet with adolescents who leave diaries open, Internet messages undeleted, and the like for parents to find. Their acts are provocative to parents and they stretch their parents' patience. It is a "no-brainer" that their parents become angry, overly protective, and vigilant. Hence, conflicting wishes of adolescents—to be separate individuals while preserving mergers with parents—are played out.

Searching for an identity with peers, they become obsessed with telephone and Internet connections. Some adolescent children experiment with same-sex partners, with whom they identify for a sense of unity. Most do not have a vocational goal that would solidify their identity. Hence, they try on new belief systems and ideologies. Adolescents often search for identity by dismissing their religious backgrounds and toying with various religions, including Wicca (the practice of witchcraft). Joining cults is an extreme version of giving up their selves for the sake of identifying with a group and worshiping a charismatic leader.

So, what is a parent to do? Love with limits is in order here. Parents need to find the balance between giving advice and letting children work it out for themselves.[2] The adolescent crisis requires patience and a sense of being anchored, as do the demands of elderly parents. To complicate matters even more, you see dreaded parts of your self in your adolescent child that you wished you had forgotten. Still another wrinkle is that you also see unwanted reflections of who you may become in your aging parent.[3]

Envy may enter the picture.[2] Many adolescent children envy their parents' freedom and power. In turn, parents envy their children's youth and spunk. Elderly, infirm parents also envy the vitality and strength of their adult children, while their adult children envy the care that parents are getting from them.

The flipside of hate is love. And the more children love their parents, the harder it is for them to separate from them.[2] Many adolescents try to make the break by resorting to rejection and rebellion. They fear gradual separation, lest they be seduced back into their former cozy, dependent identity.

The wish to be loved by parents and dependent on them is a passive style of loving. Some adolescents transform the passive style to an active style of searching for others to love them.[4] They may turn to unseemly role models in their quest for an identity. Adolescents often form tight cliques and exclude others in mean ways. If they are in the "popular" group (sexy, party animals), that becomes their "in-group," whereas the "geeks" (studious and serious) become their "out-group." Sameness and fitting in are part and parcel of finding an identity. Differences are not tolerated, as they defeat the purpose of unity and add to the sense of identity confusion.

The following case is an illustration of an adolescent in disarray.

Trying It On for Size

Madeline tearfully briefed me on her adolescent girl's provocative behavior. Lindsay was angry, sulking, pouting, and complaining. That was only half of it. Madeline found Internet pornographic conversations of Lindsay with some guy, whose email name was Slick Puppy. One of the emails was about kinky sex, a threesome and anal sex with Slick Puppy. At first, Lindsay denied it; pretty soon, in defiance, she announced that she met him in a chat room.

As though that was not enough, Madeline, a single mother of three children, was caring for her elderly father. Whereas her father had consumed her before, now her attentions were drawn elsewhere. Lindsay was in peril and Madeline's priorities shifted. Madeline was distraught and beside herself.

My surprise did not stop at Lindsay's behavior; her appearance astonished me! Her body retained the gangly look of a preteen girl. She was long legged, skinny, with a narrow build, like a nine-year-old girl. Her breasts had not developed much; neither had her sense of who she was. She wore a midriff top, skin-tight stretch pants, sparkling eye shadow, and high platform shoes and carried a designer handbag.

"I don't want to talk about what I did. That's all my mother wants to talk about. I hate her," Lindsay pouted.

"What else do you hate about your mother?" I inquired.

"She's up my butt. She's obsessed with me. I hate her." She gave me a defiant look.

"Anything else?" I was beginning to feel irked.

"She criticizes everything I do. She calls me lazy, a slut, and that she's ashamed of me." Lindsay was resistant and not taking any responsibility.

"Anything good about her?" I took another tack.

"What's good is that she has freedom and she has no one to answer to." Lindsay was envious of her mother.

"Are there things you envy about your mother?" I questioned.

"I wouldn't say that. I just want to be free like her. Instead, I'm grounded for one month. No Internet, no phone calls. I want to see Slick Puppy—his real name is Steve. I'll just sneak out and meet him." She wasn't interested in looking at her self. Instead, she was intent on blaming her mother.

"You have a strong attachment to him." I tried joining her.

"I'm in love with him." She looked dreamy.

"Do you think he's treating you with respect?" I tried once more.

"Yes, he's thoughtful and listens to all my troubles." She defended her love.

"How does that square with anal sex? Did you want it?" In my ire, two questions popped out.

"I didn't really want it. It hurt." Lindsay turned to her feelings.

"So why'd you do it?" I asked.

" I was afraid I'd lose him, so I went along with it." She looked down shyly.

"You complied with him and you rebelled against your mother," I interpreted.

"Not exactly, I was also curious. I was really curious about sex with him and another girl." I was surprised and delighted at her candor.

"So how was it?" I stayed with her.

"Not so hot. I love Steve." Lindsay was in love, or was it lust?

"What do you love about him?" I continued.

"He's exciting. He's a bad boy. He was kicked out of private school for doing drugs and for fighting." She was sounding real.

"He sounds violent. Danger can be exciting," I commented.

"I want excitement. My life's boring; school, homework, lectures from my mother, my grandfather screaming at the top of his lungs and my mother catering to him," she responded petulantly.

"It doesn't sound appealing," I agreed with her.

"No, it's not," Lindsay concurred.

"What else, other than bad boys, are you interested in?" I tried to facilitate interest in her self.

"Clothes, jewelry, and music. I want to pierce my belly button." She contemplated her belly button.

"How about sports?" I asked.

"No, I'd rather shop." Lindsay was not kidding.

"How about school?" I continued

"It's dumb." She spat that one out.

"Your mother tells me your grades have slipped. She said you were an A student," I confronted her.

"I failed some classes, and got some C's. So what! I don't care!" She dismissed me.

In the interaction with her mother, Lindsay projected her self-loathing onto her mother, and Madeline felt rejected and angry. I could feel Madeline's rage. In psychoanalytic training we learn to be aware of our feelings. Unlike parents we are not trapped by our feelings; we are able to extricate ourselves from the quagmire. When we unwittingly act on our feelings, we discuss the interaction with the patient. To facilitate change, we get in touch with repetitions of old roles and interactions. Not so when parents are embroiled with children. They are unable to step away.

Madeline felt angry about the advantages she gave her daughter. Lindsay was determined to waste the benefits bestowed on her. Madeline had her own ambitions and goals, which were on hold. Her ill father and rebellious daughter came first. Madeline's disparaging remarks and excessive curtailing of Lindsay's freedoms were related to her own feelings of helplessness and frustration. Lindsay experienced her mother's protectiveness as inhibiting her independence and sexuality. The result was angry, rebellious behavior, followed by apologies— cycles of hurt, retaliation, and repentance.

I tried confronting Lindsay with feelings we induced in each other. She would not buy it, not yet anyway. She simply wanted to defend her self. Eventually, she engaged with me in lively debates about our interactions. When I could not fight her, I joined her. We chatted about boys, clothes, jewelry, and music. She began to remark on my clothes and my appearance.

Lindsay even brought me CDs of her favorite music and asked me to listen to them. She gave me something of her self; unconsciously she did not want to separate from me. In my spare time, I listened to the music Lindsay gave me, and so she managed to stay with me.

We discussed the lyrics in her music and how she identified with the feelings. She showed me her tender side and loving feelings emerged for both of us. In some sessions, Lindsay curled up on the sofa like a cuddly kitten. We played games and giggled together. In time, she told me she no longer hated her mother and that she really loved her. We discussed her loving feelings for her mother, how she admired her strengths, raising three children alone and tending to a sick parent.

Lindsay was confused about her identity and she tried different identities on for size. Considerable time in therapy was spent on finding Lindsay's real self that was not dependent on appearances, boys or cultural images.

During adolescence, children establish a personal sense of identity or they feel identity confusion.[5] To help her establish a more unified sense of her self, we examined strengths and weaknesses, who she had been, who she was, and who she wished to be. Lindsay and I talked about relationships, her father, her parents, their divorce, and her friends.

Lindsay wanted to know about my career. I was candid about the hard work it took to derive enormous gratification. She listened and I could sense an internal shift. One day Lindsay announced that she wanted to be an archeologist. In this way she could dig up relics like a psychoanalyst. She thought that anal sex was nasty. And sex with girls was not for her. She tried it, and decided boys are better. She was still a little boy crazy, but, increasingly, her choices improved.

Lindsay's grandfather's death was followed by a period of mourning. Subsequently, Madeline went back to school. She was studying anthropology—a close cousin to archeology. Lindsay was proud of her mother. Exciting family!

YOUNG ADULTS HOLDING ON

> Human beings are the only creatures that
> allow their children to come back home.
>   Bill Cosby

Chronologically, young adults are no longer in adolescence. Emotionally and financially, however, that may be a different story. Aspects of adolescence linger on. The road to independence continues to be bumpy. I work with young adults in search of their selves—their vocational and relational identities. Some are striving to launch a career, others are away in college or graduate school, and still others are back home with their parents. And parents are muddling—often meddling—through their children's messes. Many midlife parents are also bogged down with caring for elderly parents.

Young people seeking identities need a sense of continuity and stability. In childhood, interactions with parents and family members provided continuity, security, and an identity. In young adulthood, people search for social identities outside of the family, which is fraught with instability. Their worlds are characterized by social change, divorce, and uncertainty. Colleges and careers are competitive. Jobs are scarce for young people without experience. Given the shaky economy, the future is unpredictable.

Relational mores have changed. Prom night is a marker, not necessarily for academic achievement, separating from high school, and moving on with life. It is for sexual freedom. Losing virginities by prom night is not only an imperative for boys, it is also a mandate for girls. In my youth, girls held on to their virginities until marriage. Hormones raged then and now. The big difference is the social climate. I remember when we got to know each other before sex. Now young people get to know each other after sex. Intimacy, a goal of young adulthood,[5] is open for grabs. Young people are often not emotionally mature enough for these challenges. Many are intimidated by what lies ahead. They may retreat into depression or other forms of escape, including alcohol and drugs.

Young adults seeking independence in a social climate of rapid change rely on parents for connections to the past and a sense of security. These same parents are now middle-generation children with elderly parents. Similar to young adults, aging, ill parents cling to the past and rely on their middle-aged children. Caring for two sets of children from diverse generations can be mind-blowing and backbreaking, as can be seen in the following case study.

Following in Father's Footsteps

Rick's parents were divorced when he was thirteen years old. The decision to live with his mother and elderly grandmother was easy. Rick hated his father and thought his father hated him. As for his mother, he adored her. At least that is what he professed. Nevertheless, he entered adolescence with discontinuity in his nuclear family.

Rick's father, a successful cardiac surgeon, was a tough taskmaster. Rick felt he could not do anything right for his father. In therapy, his mother Frieda came to realize that she overcompensated for his father's critical, demeaning behavior to Rick. She doted on her son. Rick could do nothing wrong; no matter what, she defended her son.

In high school, Rick had trouble with authority figures. He defied his father, the teachers, and the law. Although Rick cut classes and partied, he got good grades; it takes high intelligence to pull this off, as was the case with Rick.

At his mother's insistence, Rick, now a young adult, found his way to my office. He had bleached hair, a stubby beard, and tattooed arms. His voice was acerbic and his words often crude. All in all, Rick looked like a young tough. Underneath the rough and tough facade, I sensed a confused, but sweet young man. He was just floundering.

His fury at his father had not abated. To spite his father, Rick refused to go on to graduate school. Instead, he worked at sundry jobs—car mechanic, parking lot attendant, bouncer in a topless bar, and he dabbled in drugs. His friends were high school dropouts, stoned on drugs. High on cocaine, he and a friend broke into a house and stole a TV. They were caught. Rick was given a choice of jail or a court hearing. He chose jail. His powerful father came to the rescue and had the crime expunged from his record.

Frieda staunchly stood by Rick through thick and thin. Rick moved back home with his mother. A week later, the hospital discharged Frieda's elderly mother, who was suffering from cancer. Frieda brought her mother home with her so she would not die alone. Frieda's loyalties were split. She did not know where to turn first. I saw Frieda in adjunctive parent therapy. She came to therapy to help her son, and explained that if her son straightened out, she would be fine. And she could then deal with her mother.

"Things at home are rough. Grandma's dying, and Mom's crying all day," Rick told me.

"That sounds rough for everyone," I remarked.

"Not my dad. He's still berating my mother for how she raised me. He knows my grandma's dying. He doesn't have a heart. The weird thing is he fixes hearts for others." Rick's intelligence came through.

"It sounds like you detest your dad," I interpreted.

"He's self-righteous and arrogant. He bought off the authorities, so I wouldn't be a felon. I don't think he cared about me. It was really for him, for his high'n mighty doctor friends and his new teenybopper wife. A criminal son wouldn't look good for his image." Rick was steaming.

"So it's all about him," I reflected.

"He's an egotistical bastard." He spat out the words.

"And your mother?" I inquired.

"She's the opposite. She's unselfish, kind, and generous." The ire was gone.

"Sounds like you love her," I observed.

"She's the greatest!" His face lit up.

"Do you see any of you in your mother?" I probed his sense of himself.

"I'm sensitive like her. I love her, but I keep hurting her." Rick was real.

"Maybe things aren't so black and white. Are you like your father in any ways?" I probed further.

"I guess so, I'm smart like him," he remarked in self-wonderment.

"Perhaps you haven't found your self yet, let alone your vocational identity. It sounds like you're defining your self in rebellion against your father." I continued to probe.

"The more he's on my back, the more I mess up." Rick was seeing the light.

"And you end up hurting your self and your mother." I clarified the situation.

"I don't want to hurt her. Like I said, she's so good to me." He looked sheepish.

"Maybe she's too good. What about Cathy, whom you're seeing?" I was looking for connections.

"Cathy waits on me and has hopes for me, like my mother," he responded.

"And?" I wanted more.

"And, I treat her badly. I push her around, insult her, and she doesn't complain," Rick admitted.

"Is that how your dad treated your mother?" I dug deeper.

"Yeah. I see where you're going." He was too smart for his own good.

"Where am I going?" I asked.

"To my arrogant behavior, like my dad's." He got it.

Well, well, I thought. "What about your choice of blue-collar worker jobs? Are you sticking it to him?" I stuck it to him.

In young adulthood, Rick held on to his adolescence; his identity was inchoate. A wounded young man, Rick sought solace in all the wrong places, with all the wrong people. He split his world into good and evil, with an all-good mother and an all-bad father. Internally, he felt divided and searched for a sense of unity and continuity with his family.

In therapy, Rick began to see that his father had not only weaknesses, but also strengths. Rick got in touch with some of the reasons for hurting his mother. He found that he disdained his mother's Pollyanna attitude. He also became aware of his contempt for her subservient behavior, which, hitherto, was split off and enacted in his cruelty toward her. Once he got in touch with his unconscious motivations for hurting his mother, he was able to take control of his behavior. He confronted Frieda and they worked on their relationship in a more authentic way. Only then could Rick love his mother in a more wholesome manner. His love for his mother facilitated our relationship. When he bristled at my confrontations, we discussed our feelings. Eventually, he could see that I cared for him in totality—the good and the bad.

Before he left therapy, Rick was accepted and went off to medical school. He decided that he would outdo his father. The best revenge is a good life. His choice of friends slowly changed, and his macho behavior gave way to a gentler strength.

Frieda established a relationship with me and saw that change was in order in her relationship with Rick. No longer was he excused from egregious acts; she made sure he was accountable for them. This did not come easy, and she often slipped and pardoned him too quickly. But Frieda realized that by doing so, she was only perpetuating their mutual dependency relationship. And she was determined to make as healthy a separation from her son as he was making from her. Indeed they now have an interdependent relationship. Rick is living on campus in a nearby state and he calls his mother once a week.

Caring for her son and mother, Frieda lost touch with her female friends. Missing Rick and finding her independent self, Frieda got back in touch with her friends. One of them wanted to introduce Frieda to a widower. While Frieda was not quite ready yet, she felt excited and giddy like a schoolgirl at the prospect of new beginnings.

Separation from her mother was next. Her infirm mother was frail, silent, and in her own world. Often she did not make sense, and Frieda was in despair. She was not prepared to lose her mother, but death was drawing closer. Hence, Frieda's challenge was to separate emotionally from two people she loved dearly. After her mother died, Frieda mourned, and Rick came home from school to mourn with her.

LOVE LIFE

> Don't walk behind me, I may not lead.
> Don't walk in front of me, I may not follow.
> Just walk beside me and be my friend.
> Albert Camus

Caring for elderly parents is a central source of stress and strain on relationships.[6] A happy love and stable relationship implies a deep attachment, a capacity for mutual self-sacrifice, and a sharing in grief and pleasure, in interests, and in sexual enjoyment.[2] How can you be loving, caring, and sexy when infirm parents strain your capacities? The strain often leads to depression, exhaustion, eating problems, and other psychological problems.[7] Surely, these issues do not square with your love life. So, why do you do it? Is it a moral obligation or are the emotional bonds so strong that love relationships take a back seat? It may be some of both. Nevertheless, the family increasingly takes on the burden of elder care.[8]

Caregivers are at various phases in their relationships. Stable marriages are tested as they undergo tensions. With the additional stress, rocky relationships may be on the verge of separation. Remarriages and new relationships are strained.

A prevalent issue is the infrequency of sex in relationships. In my practice the most common sexual complaint is not the quality, but the quantity. Couples tell me, "It's great when we do it; it's just that we don't do it enough." Not only is sexual enjoyment impeded, pleasure in other areas of married life are curtailed. In a comprehensive study, fun with spouses was rare. There was no time for dinners or vacations; needy parents intruded on private time.[3]

Support from spouses is not always forthcoming. If support is available, it may be woefully insufficient. Lack of support from a spouse has decided effects on the marriage. Indeed marital satisfaction decreases when caregivers' spouses do not provide support.

Some spouses feel resentful of the time and drain on their partners. Under stress, caregivers may not reach out in a way that elicits help. Angry demands for support do not engender empathy. When needs are not met, spouses may resort to scolding their partners. Tempers flare, and they are down the slippery slope to marital distress. Even stable marriages feel shaky, as in the following case study.

Two's Company, Three's Combustible

Tipping the scales at 230 pounds, six foot three inch Zachary towered over Alice. She was petite in stature, but mighty in personality. They were an item in college. He was a football star and she was the homecoming queen. They stayed together after graduate school and married. In essence they grew up together. Alice and Zach were married thirty-eight years when Alice's father became ill and moved back into their home. The move was Alice's idea, with Zach reluctantly going along with her. Zach disliked her father and thought Alice felt the same way. She often complained that her father was stubborn, overbearing, and controlling. Alice was equally headstrong, and she fought bitterly with her father. Nevertheless, he was her father and she loved him.

"Alice wasn't easy to live with before, but now she's impossible," Zach lamented.

"Alice, how are you impossible?" I inquired.

"I ask Zach for help, not hands-on-care; I do all that. I just want consideration, some kind words. Hugs are good. Zach's just not there for me. I know him so well and he really never was. But now, I need him more than ever," Alice complained sharply.

"I'm there for you. It's you who isn't there for me. You have no time for me. When's the last time we had sex, let alone spend a quiet evening together? Your dad just has to sneeze and you're off and running," Zach countered her complaints.

"You're so selfish. He has emphysema and he may die," Alice shouted.

"Yeah, and he smokes," Zach smirked.

"It's his only pleasure," Alice defended her father.

"He's stubborn, just like you. You don't ask for help, you scold me. You're a shrew," Zach lashed out.

"You're a wimp. I need a shoulder to lean on and you cave in." Alice met his anger.

The marriage became combustible. Insults were slung back and forth. I tried to put out the flames, but failed. Finally, I held up my hand up and called "Stop."

When Alice and Zach cooled down, we discussed feelings aroused by Alice's father. Her anger was a cover for feeling helpless, drained, and exhausted. Zach was angry with Alice and her father. He resented Alice's father and the stress he brought to Alice and to their relationship. The deadlock had to be broken, which meant, for starters, that each partner set aside their ill feelings and give the marriage a chance. Next they had to see how their behavior was bringing out the worst self in their partner and not the best self.

Learning how to ask for help in a positive manner goes a long way. When Alice became aware of her feelings of helplessness, she spoke more softly and stopped blaming Zach. He began to empathize with Alice's feelings and felt remorse. And Zach gave a little more, a lot more, which Alice appreciated. As things progressed in a forward direction, they were better able to let go of the past. It was then that they could function as a team. Together they came up with creative ways to get extra help. Zach had relatives in the area and they took over the care of Alice's father for a few evening hours so that Alice and Zach had some time for a dinner or a movie. Alice reached out to her sister, who lived alone. Her sister offered to parent-sit for a weekend. Alice and Zach spent the weekend in her sister's home.

The impact of aging, ill parents spans the spectrum of married, divorced, widowed, or never-married people. A group of single people describes the impact on their lives in the following illustration.

Singles Scenes

Single people often look to new partners for a fresh start, fun, and intimacy. The intrusion of parent care feels like an impediment. Elderly, ill parents also hamper single people's wishes to socialize and to date. I hear anxious concerns about the impact of parent care on singles' relationships.

"I have no energy. When I met Eileen, I was a live wire; now I'm a washout. I'm so tired from caring for my mother that when I'm with Eileen, I fall asleep. She's going to dump me." Dennis looked exhausted.

"My mood's terrible. I want to be perky, social, and related. But I'm irritable and super sensitive. I don't have patience to hear Tom's problems. I'm full up with mine. I'm afraid I'm going to lose him." Sonia, new on the single's scene, just met someone she liked. She had trouble reviving herself to be more emotionally available.

"The nursing help had a migraine and left early. So at the last minute I had to break the date. That's not the first time. I'm scared it'll be the last time I see Roger. I'm afraid he'll leave the relationship. I can't blame him. But my mother comes ahead of Roger." Mary was rent between her mother and her boyfriend.

"So, you're all facing common dilemmas as single people. And each of you will find your own solutions. Looking back to how you coped with prior crises is helpful. Perhaps you could talk about how you coped in the past. It'll help to inspire each other," I suggested.

A dialogue ensued, with group members reminiscing, crying, laughing, and finding comfort with each other. What is more, the depressive tone in the room grew hopeful.

WORK LIFE

Caring for an elderly, ill parent is only one role for many people. Work confers yet another role for caregivers, with nearly one third of caregivers juggling roles of worker and caregiver.[6] Whether you are a professional, an employer, or an employee, you are expected to perform at the job. Work demands often compete with the needs of family, aging parents, and personal life. How many hats can you wear?

Although juggling roles of caregiver and worker is a strain, there is evidence for positive aspects of combining both roles.[6] People often find satisfactions that mediate some of their stresses. Some caregivers feel a sense of accomplishment from their jobs outside the home. For others, it is an opportunity to compensate for limitations in each role. So if you feel you are at the bottom of the totem pole at work, you may feel like a chief at home caring for a needy parent.

For some caregivers, work is a godsend. Their job is an opportunity to take a much-needed break from parents or a way to get their minds off things. Caregivers feel relief from the sad, painful situation at home. Involvement at one's job is a healthy distraction.

In many cases, caregivers do all the giving, while feeble parents are unable or unwilling to reciprocate. In the workplace, they experience reciprocal adult relationships. A work role is especially beneficial when others appreciate you, approve of your work, or validate you. Self-esteem is enhanced when you feel affirmed by others. Often, a sense of satisfaction is derived from your work. My work does wonders for me!

Other than social networks and satisfaction, there are monetary gains. Additional money is often much needed. Health insurance, paid holidays, and vacations are other benefits. These advantages may lighten your load.

COPING MECHANISMS

Feeling tossed around? Diverse role demands rocking your boat? Perhaps you could use some help to navigate these choppy waters. Here come coping mechanisms to the rescue. They will provide an anchor to stabilize your sense of self.

Coping styles may be thought of as defensive or active. Defensive coping is when people do things to protect themselves from pain brought on by death and dying.[9] Drawing on avoidance or denial is a passive approach. For a brief moment, defensive coping styles provide the illusion that troubles are diminished. Sad to say, problems do not just magically disappear because we run away from them; they only grow progressively worse. Employing active coping mechanisms entails addressing problems. Taking control of issues helps us feel in charge of our lives. And that is empowering.

Caregivers I work with who are juggling diverse role demands often feel overwhelmed. They believe their lives are running them and they don't know where to turn first. Does any of this strike a familiar chord in you? If so, untangling your self from the quagmire is essential for gaining a grip.

For starters, set up one small reachable goal that you can attain. Once you have reached that goal, pick another goal slightly harder to reach. Each incremental step that you achieve signals success. And each small success gives you the incentive to aim higher. As you unravel some of the disorder in your life, you are bound to boost your self-esteem. Goal setting may even improve your memory, as shown in a recent study.[10]

Another proactive means of empowering your self is to gather information and research the illness. The Internet is a wonderful resource, as are professionals involved with your parents' treatment. Members in psychotherapy or support groups may be informative. Psychologists working with caregivers may assist in a number of ways.

Getting involved with diagnosis and treatment helps strengthen you internally. If distance is an obstacle, you can participate by keeping in touch with the caregiver. When you feel you need a break, stop and listen to your mind and body. Distancing your self from the problem for a short time to regroup is proactive. Do not confuse temporary distance, in service of caring for your self, with avoidance.

Examine your feelings about diagnosis and treatment. You may find existential anxieties, based on fears about illness and death. These fears affect your beliefs about chemotherapy, surgery, disfigurement, or alternative therapies. Misinformation about some of these treatments sets up unfounded fears. A mastectomy, resulting in disfigurement, need not be permanent. Breast implants are a viable solution. Supplements that enhance immune systems may be beneficial. They may also have adverse interactions with other medications, which would be contraindicated. I recommend you get the real scoop from the professionals.

A healthy mind helps the body to mount a defense against disease. The correlation between mind and body is well documented. A number of psychologists and psychiatrists now specialize in gerontology. Your parents may benefit from psychotropic medication, talk therapy, or both. Imaging is one technique in which people imagine themselves as robust fighters zoning in on the diseased areas. There are numerous methods of aiding memory, including cues and lists for Alzheimer or dementia patients.

Support systems are excellent coping mechanisms. Formal support systems include transportation, nursing home care, support groups, counseling, psychotherapy, and even financial aid.[11] Informal support systems entail families and friends. Reaching out for help is another story; it may evoke strong emotional responses. I hear comments from my patients like, "I'd rather do it myself," "I can't trust anyone else," "I should take care of my parent, not a stranger," and "I feel like a cop-out if I ask for help."

People with good self-esteem are more than willing to ask for help. The belief that self-sacrifice speaks to strength is bogus. There are better ways to feel self-sufficient and robust. When you reach out to someone for help, you may be surprised to find willingness on the other end. Enlisted helpers may enjoy the prospect of being of assistance. It sure beats the helpless state of resignation of a bystander.

Once you have asked, there is the issue of accepting help. If your self-esteem is at stake, you unwittingly sabotage the help that is offered, as in Leah and Jane's case.

Sister Dear

Leah and Jane were sisters living within thirty-five minutes driving distance. Only two years apart, the sisters were raised like twins. Their mother dressed them alike until age eleven, when they wanted different clothing and hairdos. Jane was more flamboyant in her dress and Leah more conservative. Nevertheless, they remained close friends, up to a point. Their elderly mother was ill and Jane, who wasn't working, assumed the role of chief caretaker. Leah, an accountant, was busy in tax season. Nevertheless, Leah repeatedly offered to help her sister. Jane firmly refused the help.

"It's no problem. You're too busy," Jane said.

"I feel badly that you're doing all the work," Leah responded.

"It's not easy. Mostly, I don't have time to myself," Jane complained.

"I just got a new assistant, so I can get out to give you a break," Leah offered.

"I do need to have my hair done," Jane conceded.

"Do it. Just tell me when." Leah was clear about her willingness.

A date was set for Friday morning. Thursday evening Jane called Leah.

"Never mind tomorrow. The hairdresser said she'd come to my house. I can manage without you." Once again, Jane rejected Leah's help.

In therapy, Jane saw how she sabotaged the help. Leah, who was looking forward to helping out, felt rejected. Leah finally summoned her courage to tell Jane about her helpless feelings. Then, Jane felt guilty for not keeping her sister's feelings in mind.

In the past, their relationship suffered similarly, where Jane's self-sacrificing style kept Leah at a distance. Jane feared intimacy with her sister, lest she lose her individuality, reminiscent of childhood. Leah, in turn, feared rocking the boat, so she remained stuck with her feelings of resentment. Once the air was cleared, they both saw the pathos and the humor of the situation. There was no way they would regress to the earlier fused relationship. Each sister had formed a separate, full life of her own. Feeling reassured of their separateness, they found it easier to rely on each other. Jane soon found she could comfortably not only ask for help, but take it. And Leah was there to give it.

When asking for help, keep in mind that not everyone has similar proclivities or abhorrence. Some people cringe at the sight of blood, so they will not be willing to change bandages or tend to physical care of parents. Perhaps they could wash dishes or cook food. Others may be too self-absorbed to help you, so be prepared to listen to their problems. Your interest in their issues may elicit reciprocity.

It is essential that you sign up for a system that validates you. Find people with whom you can share concerns. Family members are not always ideal support figures. It may be prudent to seek support from friends, co-workers, psychotherapy group members, or a psychologist. This is a time for empathy and consolation.

Explore how you reacted to prior crises to see what worked and what did not work. Rather than allow myself to be engulfed in a maelstrom of emotions, I tend to go into action during crises. Some people wait until the dust settles before they venture forward. We are all different.

Previously, I have written about the hazards of denial. Now, I would like to revisit the subject. Denial is not always a no-no. Denial in service of passive resistance, or when used as a defense mechanism, is called negative coping. Denial can also be employed in the service of positive coping. When you feel you are losing your self, it is important to find your self. Diversion with other thoughts and activities helps you to regroup. Taking time out for friends and family is refreshing. Focusing on other interests revives your spirits.

Humor is a wonderful coping mechanism at this time. It may not be the season to be jolly, but a little levity goes a long way. A chuckle or two may do wonders for a heavy heart. You will be amazed at how uplifted you feel when you begin to laugh at yourself. Good-natured jokes that are not sarcastic may even bring smiles to dour parents.

Finally, it depends on how you look at it, as I mentioned earlier. Yes, there are losses, but there are also gains. One side of the coin has strains, burdens, and hassles. The flip side has satisfactions, pleasure, and rewards. In the process of providing care, many people derive fulfillment by realizing their ideals and values. Another reward that parent care affords is the opportunity to give back. In addition, this is a process within which you may separate, grow, and become your own individual. This pivotal experience may help you to find deeper meaning, inner fortitude, and courage.

Emotions Evoked

Some say the world will end in fire,
Some say in ice.

Robert Frost[1]

Facing feelings, rather than hiding from them, is essential for passionate living and loving. Sweeping emotions under the rug gives a tidy appearance. On the surface you look cool and collected; underneath you are seething, anxious, or depressed. Your feelings continue to fester and you risk harming your self emotionally and physically. Not only that, you may explode and harm someone you love. Indeed, heated emotions stirred up by aging parents are combustible. Erratic, out-of-control behavior gives rise to guilt and shame. Or, you may find yourself avoiding your infirm parents. Both behaviors are equally harmful. When you own dreaded feelings, you are better able to curb impulses to act in fire or in ice.

We all strive to feel vigorous and pulled together. Unfortunately, powerful emotions evoked by aging parents leave us feeling depleted and fragmented. Recognizing that negative feelings are normal is important to feel vital and cohesive. Once we embrace our dark sides, we feel more complete. We can then repair harm done and channel our undesirable feelings into desirable experiences as seen in the vignette that follows.

Hide and Seek

Jeri, a plump woman, with a double-chinned baby face and short gray hair was rummaging through her oversize handbag. She pulled out some pictures of herself taken only seven years ago. The group was astounded; Jeri was a knockout! Now Jeri soothed her jangling nerves with carbohydrates.

" 'The food's too hot, too cold, too sweet, too spicy.' That's all I hear. I feel like shoving it down her throat. Instead, I shove it down mine. Last night I couldn't take it, so I polished off a box of chocolate chip cookies. Like that wasn't bad enough, I binged even more with a pint of chocolate ice cream. The skinnier she gets, the fatter I get," Jeri cried out for help.

"My mother also wants the impossible and I can't come through. I feel helpless," Marilyn empathized with Jeri.

"Yeah, I guess I feel helpless. I can't believe it. I was so independent. I left my alcoholic husband years ago, worked as a teacher, and raised five kids single handed." Jeri brightened up when she recalled her strengths.

"Does it help you to eat?" Jonathon, a slim, well-built man asked.

"It helps to fill me in. I feel empty, depressed, and worthless. And I'm always on edge." Jeri was discouraged.

"I also feel depressed and anxious; it's not only about my frail mother. It's about my son, who has marital problems," Sandy offered.

"Me too. My grown daughter's in trouble and needs me," Jeri joined Sandy.

"I get angry a lot. My wife says I have an anger management problem. So, I went into therapy. She was right. I'm learning how to control my anger," Jim proudly announced.

"How do you do that?" Sandy was interested.

"I try to be more assertive and I don't comply when I don't want to. I get a lot of tension out on the tennis court. You should see my backhand." Jim shared his prowess.

"I don't feel angry, I just feel frustrated." Jeri's dangerous feelings were in hiding.

"Jeri, you're just too nice. You always say the right thing at the right time." Max was perceptive and somewhat sarcastic.

"I try to be a good person and take care not to harm others," Jeri said demurely.

"You're just too good to be true." Max was bound to get to Jeri. His anger was out there.

"We all want to be nice people, but we may have feelings that aren't so nice. That doesn't make us bad people. I've found that when we hide from our anger, it's got to come out somewhere. Either we explode or implode. Both ways are hurtful. Max shows his anger. Jim is trying to channel his anger. I wonder whether men are more comfortable owning their aggression than women. Jeri's anger went underground and is doing its damage. Anger turned inward may be the root of her depression and anxiety. " I summarized some observations and thoughts to the group.

A lively debate ensued. The female group members sought, then found, real voices. They began to speak up in more forceful ways. The women had it in them; they just needed permission and encouragement to express their split-off feelings of aggression. Asserting themselves, rather than hiding from their feelings, was the catalyst to more empowered and lively experience.

IDENTIFYING FEELINGS

Dueling Feelings

Caring for elderly, ill parents may leave you feeling sad, depressed, anxious, irritable, and angry.[2,3] These feelings are fairly easy to identify. Other feelings are unconscious and less obvious. Many caregivers report feeling confused, depleted of energy, and stressed; they are unaware of conflicting feelings—dual feelings that wage battle within psyches, give rise to emotional distress and loss of energy. And love may give way to rage, respect to disdain, caring to neglect, feeling helpful to feeling helpless, and joy to sadness. Harboring divergent feelings is normal; it does not mean you are a messed-up or malevolent person.

Feelings that duel have a long history. Melanie Klein wrote that the struggle between love and hate, with all its conflicts of guilt, self-loathing, and reparation, began in infancy and is active throughout life.[4] More recently, Stephen Mitchell compared the intense feelings of love and hate in adulthood to that of love and hate in childhood relations with parents.[3]

What is more, love finds further definition in the presence of hate,[5] just as altruism does in selfishness, gratitude in envy, and resurrection in destruction. Without dark moments to offset the bright ones, we would have dull, gray inner landscapes. There are no mountain peaks without valleys—only flat lines.

Aggression

I have found that the topic of aggression is touchy. When I bring up the subject, I inevitably get strong responses. Some people wish to avoid aggression at all costs and clam up. Others can hardly wait to sink their chops into someone. What is it about aggression? How does aggression arise? Theorists over the years have tried to explain the roots of aggression. Is it wired into our hardware? Is it a primitive bestial vestige? Or is it learned from our environment?

Sir Thomas Hobbes, an early British philosopher, wrote about the state of nature as chaotic, brutal, wolf against wolf, man against man.[6] He believed that our natures were violent and predatory. Jean-Jacques Rousseau, a Frenchman, held a contradictory position. He posited that human beings were benign and social by nature, and that if environments were favorable, people would live in harmony.

Dollard and Miller and colleagues,[7] American behaviorists, ushered in a psychological era of locating the causes of behavior in learned experiences. The frustration/aggression hypothesis contends that aggression is related to the deprivation we feel when benign experiences are thwarted. Hence, feelings of deprivation lead to feelings of frustration, which in turn are expressed as aggression. Your aging parents feel frustrated about their inability to care for themselves. They may also feel deprived of health, vitality, and youthfulness. In turn, you may feel frustrated and deprived of a life of your own. Aggression, whether turned inward or outward, is the result.

Harry Stack Sullivan, the founder of the interpersonal school of psychoanalysis, had other views of aggression. He believed aggression was an innate means of protection from anxiety. When we fear danger or threats, we draw on aggression as a survival mechanism.[8]

Ailing parents feel endangered, especially when they undergo surgery and noxious chemotherapy and experience pain. Anger is employed as a survival technique in response to threats of disease. Some elderly people feel depressed, powerless, and fearful, so they draw on aggression for a temporary fix. Anger is a great antidote for depression and weakness. For a brief moment they roar like mighty lions and fend off the scared mice inside.

Aggressive, harsh parents leave scars on small, helpless, dependent children. Children may transform themselves from the powerless role, by taking on the role of the powerful aggressor. Psychoanalysts refer to this process as "identification with the aggressor." This turnabout may become violent if power is abused.

Although aggression is a component of every one of us, it does not mean we have to express it with cruel acts. Transforming aggression to assertion is a healthier avenue for expression. No doubt, the betterment of humankind comes to mind when you think of Mahatma Gandhi. Then there is Nelson Mandela, who freed a people from apartheid. These two Nobel Peace Prize winners utilized their aggression to lead nonviolent and powerful revolutions.

Aggression is not always overt. Neglect or dismissal is as hurtful as insults or bodily assaults. Child abuse is not only enacted when parents physically abuse children; neglect is also a form of child abuse. The Amish use communal shunning as a severe form of punishment.

Hostile acts, committed sneakily or behind someone's back, are called passive-aggressive behaviors. These acts are cowardly ways of running away from problems. Some people would just as soon lie to their partners as meet them head-on. Rather than tackle issues directly about the relationship, some people withdraw into work, gambling, or substance abuse, or they may cheat on their partners. Hence, direct confrontation is avoided; however, the hurtful bell of hostility rings loud and clear as seen in the following case.

A Balancing Act

Beverly and Charles were married fifteen years. It was the second time around for both of them. Beverly was a tall, husky, smartly dressed woman. Charles was short, pudgy, and unshaven. His casual printed sports shirt was open to his belly. Beverly was a hotshot real estate agent, and Charles was a laid-back golf pro. Whereas her tailored pumps matched her attire, his bare feet were covered with worn leather sandals. They were, indeed, from different schools of thought. Problems were there from the beginning, only to worsen recently.

When Beverly's aging mother was too ill to live alone, they decided to move her into their home. Beverly felt stressed and wanted more attention and support from Charles, which was not forthcoming. She had to cajole, nag, and resort to threats for Charles to respond. Charles managed to find time for his three grown children and grandchildren from his ex-wife. Their fights escalated and their love life diminished. Although their fighting styles were at two opposing poles, they balanced each other with their aggression.

"Charles is a washout. Golf comes first, then his kids. I come last. I'm stressed and worn out from my mother, and I need support," Beverly spoke plaintively.

"You're too uptight about everything, complaining, nagging me. I can't stand it." Charles tried to stay calm.

"If you were in the least empathic, I'd relax. You're a mean bastard," Beverly cried out in anger.

"And you're a bitch. I'm sick and tired of your insults," Charles shouted back.

"I'm sick and tired of how your kids treat me. They call and hang up when I answer. Or they ask to talk to you without even acknowledging me. You've done nothing to facilitate our relationship." Beverly was weeping.

"They're adults and I can't do anything to change their minds. Get over it," Charles snapped back.

"I wish I could get over you. Maybe that's what you want?" Beverly attacked.

"I don't get it. I don't cheat on you, drink, or beat you." Charles bemoaned his fate.

"You're right, it's not what you do; it's what you don't do that hurts so much." Beverly hit home and Charles winced.

"Yeah, well your insults and anger hurt more," Charles defended himself.

Clearly Beverly and Charles were enraged with each other. Beverly felt frustrated and deprived. She belted out her aggression for all to hear. Charles felt belittled and his manhood was threatened. His aggression was passive and hid behind the scenes. Their daggers differed, but their aggression was on an even par.

Therapy was long and tedious, with stops and starts. Their styles of relating, with a long history in childhood, had undergone revisions. Unfortunately, with the additional stress of Beverly's ill mother, old patterns resurfaced. Each partner felt he or she was in the right and insisted on blaming the other. Neither was willing to own the aggression. Beverly insisted her rage was warranted, and Charles felt he was only reacting to her onslaughts. They continued defending themselves. I explained that they were not in court and did not have to defend themselves, and that it was a waste of everyone's time. The goal of marital therapy is for each person to own his or her role in the conflict, rather than look to the other person for culpability.

The couple embarked on a healing journey, bringing fun into the marriage and revitalizing their love. By pleasuring each other, their differences did not loom as large, and they could then empathize with each other. Intertwined with the healing process they addressed underlying problems. Was Charles to continue ducking or to get involved? With more love expressed in the marriage, Charles felt safe to be more involved and stand up to his children. Was Beverly to continue yelling or give Charles a chance to prove what he was capable of? Upon recording herself, Beverly was stunned by her ugly responses to Charles. She decided to pipe down and draw on her gentler side. The dynamic slowly changed.

Karen's story, which follows, is a mother-daughter case of differing expressions of aggression.

Two Faces of Fury

A normally soft-spoken woman, Karen was raising her voice lately. As a social worker, she was busy caring for other people's welfare. As a daughter, caring for her mother's welfare fit the profile. Although they had a long history of friction, Karen felt duty bound to keep close watch on her elderly mother.

"She's driving me crazy," Karen complained

"What's she doing?" I inquired.

"She clings to me and cries for constant attention. I have other responsibilities and I lose my patience with her. I'm mean to her. Then I feel guilty." Karen looked sullen.

"So, you're furious. Do you think your mother's furious?" I inquired.

"I wouldn't call her furious. She shuts down and won't talk to me. Last night I called her repeatedly, but she wouldn't answer. I started to imagine she was lying dead on the floor. So, I ran over there. She was fine, watching TV, laughing, and having a good old time. " Karen was seething.

"So she punishes you and gets what she wants in the end," I interpreted.

"Yeah, she gets my goat. It'd be so much easier if she just let me have it. The silent treatment is far worse," she protested.

"So, you wish she'd be more direct with her anger, like you," I mirrored her.

Karen and her mother both felt angry. Her mother's aging and death were threatening, so she clung to Karen. When Karen disappointed her, she screamed out silently. Her mother's aggression was disguised, but it was there—another example of passive-aggressive behavior. Karen's aggression was forthright and candid. Either style had the same painful effect.

Karen's challenge was to relinquish the illusion that her mother would change. Their conflict had roots in early childhood, when Karen wanted more of her mother's attention. She recalled how over the years her mother was in her own head, ignoring Karen, talking right over her, and continuously disappointing her. Relinquishing a long-held illusion gave way to mourning a painful loss. Her mother had abandoned her many years ago, and would continue to do so until the final abandonment—death. After mourning the loss of the illusion that her mother would change, Karen engaged in a more objective and compassionate perspective of her.

Aggression that is acknowledged is less of an anathema than when it is denied or disowned. Committing hostile acts with impunity is not what I am talking about. Neither is cloaking aggression in the hood of sweetness and innocence. Blaming the other person for your disavowed aggression leaves you at the mercy of that person. You are unwittingly transferring your power to them, evacuating your self, and leaving you weakened. You cannot control anyone else's behavior—only your own.

Taking responsibility for aggression allows you to have options. An empowering choice is to transform anger into assertion. Speaking out on issues dear to your heart, meeting challenges in relationships, healthy competition, creative endeavors, and satisfying work are powerful, peaceful ways to reclaim your self.

EMOTIONAL IMPACT

Many adult children volunteer to care for elderly, infirm parents simply because they love them; they feel a close, warm attachment to their parents. Researchers who observed infant-mother attachments wrote about the consequences for later life.[9,10] They found an enduring bond established in early childhood was a close emotional tie that continued throughout the life span, and provided the foundation for later relationships.[11,12] A recent study of caregivers supported the continuity of the attachment theory.[11] Adult children's helping behaviors and commitment to continue helping were related to dependency feelings by elderly parents. So the attachment continued, but the direction changed. Whereas in earlier years, dependent young children elicited help from parents, now dependent elderly parents elicited help from their adult children.

Not all ties, however, remain loving. Feelings of obligation or a sense of duty underlie some helping behavior. The daughter-mother tie and the conflict have been well documented; however, the daughter–elderly father tie has not been.[12] Freud understood the conflict between adult children and aging parents up close. He had the opportunity to observe his adult patients providing care for their elderly parents, as well as his own conflicted experience of caring for his ailing father.[13]

Oedipal Conflict Revived

Freud examined the role of early childhood wishes on later life. He theorized that the Oedipal wish (attraction to the opposite-sex parent and rivalry with same-sex parent) was revived in adult life. He posited that unconscious incestuous wishes were exacerbated during the stressful role of caring for an elderly parent.

While the Oedipal myth is based on sons' unconscious forbidden wishes for their mothers, the bulk of Freud's patients were women. The supposition for women is that attraction to their fathers results in rivalry with their mothers. The forbidden incestuous wishes give rise to guilt. Freud held that unconscious incestuous wishes were at the root of a severe mental illness in women, known as conversion hysteria.[13]

In Freud's "talking cure," women free-associated and became aware of their unconscious wishes. Finally, women resolved their guilt by transferring forbidden love to a suitable man with whom they could have a loving, sexual relationship. According to this principle, the rivalry set up with mother continues unless it is brought to awareness and transformed to cooperation and healthy competition with other women. The same idea applies to men, except that sexes are reversed. Hence, men harbor incestuous wishes for their mothers and compete with their fathers and other men.

Freud believed that feelings of competition and resentment conflicted with feelings of concern and tenderness. This conflict continued throughout the life span, including the complex tie between middle-age children and their elderly parents. In my practice, I have observed similar emotional bonds and binds.

When fathers and daughters have close, emotionally erotic relationships, daughters are competitive and resentful of their mothers or other women. Again, the same holds true for mothers and sons. Emotionally erotic relationships do not necessarily entail sexual abuse, but there are consequences. The effects of sexual abuse are pernicious and far beyond the scope of this book.

Separation and Individuation

No matter the loving or dutiful feelings, providing care for elderly, frail parents evokes frightening and painful emotions. The difficult process, however, provides an opportunity to resolve previously unresolved struggles around separation and individuation[14] (becoming a separate, independent individual). The childhood wish for merger with parents is universal and is intensified by the impending loss of parents.

In the Speilberg film, *A.I.* (for artificial intelligence), a robot child adheres to the illusion of merger and bliss with his mother. He never grows up and embarks on an endless search for Eden—reunion with his mother. Molly Walsh Donavon interprets the Greek myth of *Demeter and Persephone* as a tale of mother-daughter relationship vicissitudes. Donavon speculates that the wish to be a separate person is threatening and that merger is maintained by inhibiting growth and development.[15]

I have found that anorexic adolescent girls and their mothers have deep-seated dissonant feeling about separation. Proclaiming their independence, many girls show behaviors that contradict their assertions. They retreat from physical and emotional growth. Rather than deal with the outside world, they stay close to home and obsess about food and their bodies. The result is reunion with mother, childlike bodies, and arrested development.

Adult children caring for elderly parents are reunited by circumstances. At a deeper level, reunion with mother may be a form of unconscious fantasy to merge with mother,[14] to have close bodily contact with parent, and for her to nurse you. The infant-mother attachment was paradise. Merger now, however, brings fears of engulfment. Whether frail or feisty, elderly parents keep adult children closely tied to them. Hence, desire for and fear of fusion clash.

This may well be an ideal time to have the best of both worlds. Aside from vicissitudes, ministering to mother's needs represents a second chance for a close bodily and emotional connection without the real threat of an engulfing union that would be antithetical to separation.[14] Whether the reunion is engulfing or empowering depends on how you handle the situation. No doubt, you are tugged to abandon your self and sacrifice your independence. Breaking that important appointment is easier than breaking away from a complaining, ill parent. But is that in your parent's or in your best interest?

You may also find yourself distancing or disengaging from parents. Devoid of power, racked with pain or loss of bodily and cognitive functions, dying parents may evoke overwhelming anxieties about your fate. You fear that you will suffer a similar death.[14] Existential angst and close identification with parents may deter your capacity to relate with compassion.

A prior relationship of friction complicates the process of care. The unrequited wish to be accepted, loved, and in union with parents resurfaces when elderly parents continue to reject and condemn adult children. As old issues bubble up, it helps to reexamine their meaning and import in the current relationship. It may be time to let go and to move on.

Although you fear your parents will devour you, your sense of autonomy is not really at risk. Step back, observe their weak and fragile states, and you will be in a better place to tolerate their slights. Infirm, aged parents do not have the strength to be effective anymore. Their powerlessness belies the imagined powers they once had over you. Instead of feeling threatened, feelings of concern and tenderness may emerge. And the process of separation and individuation has begun, as in Felicia's case.

Felicia in Flight

Felicia had a history of discord with her mother, related to Oedipal and separation issues. At age seventeen, she left home to live in a commune. She then went on to become an antiestablishment social activist fighting for indigenous people, civil rights, and more recently, animal rights. Throughout her life she kept in close contact with her mother, who sent her much-needed money. Felicia appreciated the financial help, but she experienced her mother as disapproving, judgmental, and rejecting. Felicia ran not only from her mother, but also from her self. Slowly, she drifted into mainstream society and got a job working in a veterinarian's office close to her beloved animals.

Her mother died recently, and Felicia was distressed. Her mother's death was painful to watch, as she withered away in a hospice. Felicia visited her mother, and although she ached for her, she recalled that she could hardly wait to leave.

"I feel terrible, like I'm a bad, horrid person." Felicia lowered her head, and her long gray hair hid her face.

"Why's that?" I asked.

"I couldn't stand her. I tried to talk with her, but she looked away in disdain. I can't believe she still condemned me. She told me I wasn't dressed right. I was wearing a skirt and a top like I'm wearing now. Do you see anything wrong with that?" Her sadness gave way to ire.

"You look fine." I checked out her long denim skirt, floral printed shirt and bushy gray hair. She reminded me of the flower children of the sixties.

"What does she want with me? Aside from criticism, she's wanted nothing to do with me. She may have loved me, but she definitely didn't like me. Different story for my brother; he's always been the love of her life." Felicia looked sullen.

"How about your Dad?" I was curious.

"I was Dad's favorite. But, I still wanted Mom." Felicia's candor was refreshing.

"Have you always longed for her approval?" I probed.

" I don't know. I was pathetically shy as a little girl," she responded.

"Maybe you were depressed," I suggested.

"I remember that I was always angry with her. As an adolescent, I rebelled and ran wild." Felicia's fire was lit.

"What was her response? " I asked.

"She denounced me and lauded my brother. You know the sad part of it is that I love her." Her dark eyes closed as she sighed.

"Have you told her that?" I inquired.

"Yeah, just before she died, I said, I love you, Mom. She didn't respond. So, I asked her if she loved me. She looked away and remained silent. Even on her deathbed she couldn't say I love you." Felicia sobbed loudly and I felt her despair.

As an adolescent girl, Felicia suffered from a premature separation. A psychologically unequipped child, Felicia catapulted herself into pseudo-adulthood. She refused to comply with her mother's traditional values and rebelled. Underlying her depression and rage was the unrequited love for her mother. She longed for reunion and merger with her mother of infancy, which she perceived as the happiest time of her life. The futile fantasy was sadly revived with her mother's death.

The therapy revolved around healing from unresolved issues, Felicia's unrealistic wishes for merger and her unhealthy responses to the frustration. We plunged into depths that were daunting. I admired Felicia for her courage, creativity, and intelligence. An adventurous adolescent and young woman, Felicia was temporarily stuck in midlife. She revived the old spirit, drew on her strengths, and embarked on a challenging road of renewal. Separating from old scripts and becoming a strong individual were on the map. After obtaining her degree as a veterinarian, she opened her own office.

WAYS TO AFFIRM YOUR SELF

Stormy emotions and discordant feelings run amuck. You may have suffered from depression, anxiety, or other emotional problems in the past. If so, you feel the impact more than other people. Negative comparisons to others, who are seemingly coping while you are shedding copious tears, only deflate you further. Positive feedback from others enhances your self-esteem and develops a more sturdy sense of self.

In the Felicia case, she elicited genuine feelings of love and validation from me when she began to take responsibility for her off-putting behaviors. Things often got dicey, but she did not run away as she did in the past. We discussed the enactments in the therapy relationship and great strides were made. Felicia not only desired but sorely needed the authentic admiration of a woman who would affirm her self in entirety, with all its good and not so good aspects.

My experience with Felicia reminds me of a recent study of later-life women. In this study, researchers examined the effect of self-enhancing evaluations and of feedback from others.[16] Self-enhancing evaluations occurred when women perceived themselves as faring well compared to others in similar circumstances. There was marked improvement in psychological health when women saw themselves in a favorable light compared to others. Perceiving positive feedback from others also indicated a decrease in depressive symptoms.

I am all for finding a support system in which your needs are met. Seek others who appreciate and affirm you. Warm loving environments, like-minded supportive friends, family members, co-workers, and therapy groups are productive paths to psychological health. Psychologists/psychoanalysts, who love you in totality, facilitate emotional development and feelings of self-worth.

Dark Feelings
in the Spotlight

This is the very worst wickedness, that we refuse to
acknowledge the passionate evil that is in us.
This makes us secret and rotten.

D. H. Lawrence

In heaven all the interesting people are missing.

Friedrich Nietzche

We all like to feel good about ourselves and believe that we are
well-meaning people. What about dark feelings toward parents? Are
they forbidden because you feel they are wrong? Does that make
you a bad person? As social beings, moral conscious guides our
sense of right or wrong. Without a sense of morality, we don a veil
of impunity for evildoing. Although people with sociopathic personalities may fear punishment by the law, they lack an inner moral
conscious to guide their behavior. Some people distort morality to
justify evil acts. In the name of religion, fundamentalist suicide
bombers rationalize murder.

Evolution as human beings would be decidedly arrested if we had
not developed a moral consciousness, known by analysts as a superego.
Good things, however, may go awry. When we are unduly hard on our
selves, torturing our selves with unwarranted guilt, the superego becomes harsh and punitive. Negative feelings toward aging, infirm
parents give rise to self-blame. Hating parents is a dark feeling, even
when these parents are emotionally and verbally abusive. Wishing
them forever silenced or dead feels worse. Guilty feelings go along with
the territory. I would like to underscore that feelings are not synony-
mous with actions. Feelings are just feelings, and we have many that
contradict each other.

Paradox is an integral part of humanity. Life gives birth to death, sun to shade, and oceans to shores. Full, rich experience requires the heights of ecstasy and the depths of misery. We cannot fully immerse ourselves in feelings of love, respect, or gratitude without, at times, experiencing the dark undersides of hate, shame, and envy.

TABOO FEELINGS

The emotional impact of taboo feelings on adult children is intense. At an early age, we have been inculcated with a social mandate to respect our elders. We are taught to honor thy mother and father. So, how does that square with your dark feelings and loathsome fantasies? Killing your parent is, indeed, patricide. Wishing them dead is not patricide; it is a fantasy. There is a big difference. Fantasies and feelings do not have to translate to actions. In order for you to take control of your emotions, it is essential to be aware of them, no matter how despicable.

Feeling frustrated and enraged, adult children often wish their parent's death. But, they do not act on those feelings. Yet, many punish themselves with suffering and guilty feelings, as though they are culpable of evildoing.[1]

Psychoanalysts explore wishes and fantasies, as well as reality. Melanie Klein wrote that infants have death wishes against unyielding mothers. In infancy, babies believe that their hateful feelings have come true and they have destroyed their mothers. Love overcomes hate, so that infants feel guilty and wish to repair mothers. Hence, Melanie Klein placed the genesis of the superego at this early pre-Oedipal stage of development. And she held that very early conflict between love and hate was the root of feelings of guilt and unworthiness, which remained active all through life.[2] In the following vignette, group members reveal detested feelings.

Shame on Me

"She took such good care of me when I was young. I was a handful; she didn't have it easy. It's my turn now. I have an obligation to pay back. Only, I don't want to do it. I just want to get away from her," Ralph, a shy, soft-spoken man murmured to the group.

"Me, too, then I feel terrible. It's a sin to dishonor your parents. I dishonor him when I don't assume my share of the burden. I avoid him. I can't stand to look at his deteriorating body. My younger sister does all the care, and I feel guilty. I value fairness and what I'm doing isn't fair to my mother or to my sister," Amy wailed.

"You think that's bad. I know it's my duty to care for him, and I don't want to. He's abusive, insults me, and curses me out. I find myself wishing he'd die already. That's so bad." Sal was sad.

"When he gets that mean look on his face and strikes out at me in a fury, I forget how fragile and ill he is. I find myself waiting for him to fall asleep so I can rest. Lately I say to myself 'die already so I can live.' Then I detest myself. I hate hating him. It's a big taboo for me. I'm supposed to love him and feel sorry for him," Lisa sighed.

"My dad isn't mean or abusive; he's considerate. Unfortunately, he's frail and dying, so I really feel like a heel when I don't visit. He was my hero and it's hard to face that I'm losing him. I feel very guilty." Harold's eyes filled with tears.

"You're lucky your dad's so considerate. My mother makes me crazy and I lose my cool. I told her I hated her. She cried and I felt so small. I hated my self," Barbara joined Lisa.

"I know what you mean. I loathe my father; then I loathe myself. As a child, he worked two jobs and gave us kids everything. Now he's stubborn, raging, and controlling. I should be a bigger person, but I feel like a lowdown worm, " Danny joined the others.

"I shouldn't feel as I do. She's responsible for my success in life. She worked herself to the bone to give me an education, clothes on my back, food in my mouth. My dad was a deadbeat, and my mom did it all single-handed. I should feel grateful and loving toward her. Sometimes I do, but other times. Wow! The sparks fly." Sharon hung her head in shame.

"I hear a lot of shoulds and moral imperatives. You're trying to push unwanted feelings underground, but they're flourishing. It seems to me that you feel shame, guilt, and a lot of anguish. What's more you're torturing your selves unjustly. Feelings aren't behaviors. Indeed, by being aware of hateful feelings, we can take control and be careful not to act on them. Splitting them off can be dangerous, as you are more apt to act on them unwittingly." I gave permission to bring dark, forbidden feelings into the light for closer scrutiny.

LOSING IT

So, you lashed out and lost it. You are not alone. Adult children do lose it. Even though they love their parents, caretakers may react in hostile ways to demanding, abusive elderly parents. Love-hate relationships are widespread. Expressing justified hate may be a loving act. In a renowned psychoanalytic paper, D. W. Winnicott described his experiences with a child whom he took into his home and cared for. Despite his love for the boy, when the boy was loathsome, Winnicott expressed his hate directly to him. In this authentic way, the child, by experiencing hate, could also arrive at love.[3]

Current trends in psychoanalysis emphasize the centrality of analysts' feelings toward their patients, which we call countertransference. Many of our patients induce hateful feeling in us, as they did with their parents and others. Psychoanalysts are trained to be in touch with our dark feelings, so that we do not react in retaliatory ways. There are times when our feelings are not in check. Unwittingly, we react harshly, as others have. Together, patient and analyst enact familiar abhorrent patterns of relating. In the analysis, a discussion follows, so that patients learn about their behavior and how they enlist others to do dirty work. We are trained to use our countertransference, which is not the case when caring for elderly parents.

Unchecked anger is agonizing for your parents and for you. The warring dynamics in the relationship may be based on old battles, heightened by current skirmishes. Your impasse stems from conflicting needs of caring for parents while attending to other obligations. Your parents' plight centers mainly around their illness and death. They are too ill to think about the impact on you.

GETTING A GRIP

> If you haven't forgiven yourself something,
> How can you forgive others?
>   Dolores Huerta

Loving relationships go awry in the face of intense conflict and pressure. Rational thinking and empathic relating give way to miscommunication and irrational behavior. To get a grip, you must first forgive your self. Self-forgiveness strengthens you to arrive at a place of understanding and compassion. If you are busy hating your self, you are apt to foreclose tender communication and sympathy. Self-loathing is wasted energy. It only brings self-pity and more pain. Desperate for relief from these dreaded emotions, you may strike out and blame your parent.

There is a vast divide between blaming your self and taking responsibility. Blaming your self is enfeebling and leads to depression. Taking responsibility affords you the opportunity to change your behavior. In doing so, you are fortified with greater buoyancy to survive the storm.

In my work, uncovering the wounded child within a depressed, anxious, or raging patient helps me feel compassion. It may work for you, too. Review childhood injuries of your parents and of your self. You will be more prepared to take responsibility for loss of control. Then you may choose to make reparations with kinder and gentler care. Guilty feelings are mitigated and your parents may well enjoy your ministrations, so that the entire interaction changes. Sandra's story illustrates how she found compassion for her inner child and for her hurtful mother.

Sandra's Sad Saga

Sandra's ex-husband was self-involved and cruel, and the world turned around him. She tried in vain to please him, and after thirty-two years of marriage, Sandra finally gave up. She divorced him and moved into her own apartment. Her widowed mother lived in the same town.

"I got this cute apartment and I love the peace and quiet. But it wasn't meant to be. My mother's giving me a hard time. Come to think of it, she was always difficult." Sandra contemplated her dilemma.

"How's that?" I asked.

"As far back as I can remember she was vain and self-centered. It was always about her." Sandra searched her past experience to get some clarity about the present.

"She's like your first husband. You've told me how self-involved he was," I said.

"Yeah, I married my mother. They're not only vain; they're both stubborn and unreasonable. I'm such a fool. My mother knows exactly what buttons to push." Her tone took on a harsh quality.

"How does she do that?" I inquired.

"I can't do enough for her. She wants to consume every waking moment of mine. I had a dream last night. I dreamed about a spider. It's about my mother, she's pulling me into her web," Sandra interpreted, and went on with her story.

"Mom was hospitalized last week with her heart. The cardiologist loves skinny, but he said she was dangerously anorexic. It's no wonder she's emaciated; she doesn't eat. It makes me so mad. We get into big screaming fights over it. She's so stubborn." Sandra was frustrated and angry.

"How about you? Are you stubborn?" Sandra was overweight, with high blood pressure, both risk factors for a heart attack. Each time I broached her health Sandra blew me off with, "OK, OK, I know I'm rebelling against my skinny mother. So what, you only live once." Like her mother, Sandra was defensive and obstinate.

"I guess I'm stubborn," she admitted.

"Do you counterattack?" I hoped that that she would look at her self.

"I do. But she starts it. She's impossible." Sandra was not assuming any responsibility yet.

"So she starts, but you continue." I stayed the course.

"I can't help myself. She's frustrating me and making me sick. You know I have heartburn and high blood pressure and I'm overweight. I swear she's the culprit; my body's falling apart, not to mention my mind. I feel like I'm going crazy." Sandra sounded helpless.

"So, you feel frustrated and angry. Do you feel helpless?" I was beginning to feel helpless in trying to reach her.

"Yeah, I feel helpless. She refuses to live with me, but she still wants me to look after every one of her whims. I gave her a portable phone to carry around with her, but she won't turn it on. I called her for two days and she didn't answer, so finally I went over to see how she was. She told me she fell, hurt her knee, and there was no one to help her. I told her that if she'd answer the phone, I would've come to help her. So what does she say? She says 'I'm nauseous, bring me a cup of tea.' I made the tea and then she complained that other children always make tea for their parents and they take them out to dinner. I screamed back, 'What's the point of taking you to dinner when you don't eat?' So, she screamed back that she had no appetite and that I didn't care about her." Sandra sighed heavily.

"It does sound like you're both short on understanding, communicating, and compassion. What's more, you feel like a victim." I summed up some of the themes I heard.

"First my ex-husband and now mother. I sure have lousy luck." Sandra was wallowing in self-pity.

"So your sad saga continues," I commented.

"I feel ashamed of myself. I want to love her, but she doesn't let me." She was not attending to my comment.

"A lot of us have a parent we love and hate. Tell me about her childhood." I joined her and moved the dialogue to her mother. I have found that fighting with patients in order to get my point across is futile. Interestingly, a parallel dynamic was happening with Sandra and her mother; her fight with her mother was also futile. I changed directions and moved into a more empathic union.

"She was orphaned at an early age and raised by her grandmother," Sandra recounted.

"So she had a major early traumatic loss," I interpreted.

"Yeah, she did. She had little education, but was very beautiful. She told me that a million times. That's why my father married her," Sandra continued her mother's story.

"Maybe she felt deficient because she relied on her looks. And now they're gone. She's probably angry at her fate," I inferred.

" I hadn't thought of it that way before. I remember how preoccupied my mother was with appearances. How things looked to the neighbors was more important than spending time with me. She was superficial and never liked me because I wasn't pretty like her." Tears welled up.

"So, where'd you get your prettiness?" I suspected poor self-esteem. Despite her plumpness, Sandra was appealing. She had a charming dimpled smile with a peaches-and-cream complexion.

"From nobody. I'm ugly. I wasn't lucky there either." She confirmed my suspicion.

"It sounds like both of you suffered losses and pain. She believes she lost her beauty, which is a blow to her fragile self-esteem. You lost out on two counts. You lost the illusion of unconditional love, and you lost a clear reflection of your self. You see your self in your mother's distorted mirror." I addressed mutual losses and pain.

"She's a lost soul and so am I." Sandra broke down. Her stout shoulders shrunk as she caved in sobbing.

In subsequent sessions, Sandra arrived at greater clarity and compassion for her mother and her self. She moved from a helpless victim, blaming fate and other people, to a more robust survivor. As such, she was able to assume accountability; soon she felt it was time to forgive her mother. Invitations to dinner were extended, whether or not her mother ate. Sandra even took her mother to see a sad Broadway show and they both had a good cry.

Guilt, Guilt, and More Guilt

> Guilt and self-pity have a complex relationship.
> Sometimes they are locked together in a zero-sum game;
> the more there is of one, the less there is of the other.
>   Stephen A. Mitchell[1]

GUILT PANGS

Even though they are doing the utmost to help, and rationally they know they are, somehow my patients still suffer from guilt pangs. Some of my group members plaintively cry out in agony.

Group in Guilt

"How can I enjoy the ballet when she can't even walk?" Suzanne, a depressed caregiver, was trying to lift up her spirits. She was a dedicated daughter, who spent an inordinate amount of time with her sick mother.

"Enjoy. It'll make her happy to know you're working on your depression," Bonnie reassured Suzanne.

"I know that, but I still couldn't stay. I left the ballet early." Suzanne looked dejected.

"When you told us about the ballet last week, you cheered up. Now you look sadder than ever." Bonnie was observant.

"Maybe you feel ashamed of yourself. I know I do. Last night I had sex with my hubby and it was great! Now I feel like I was selfish." Marianne's joy soured overnight.

"You're lucky you have a sex partner. The only partner I have is my father. He's not exactly my sex partner; he's my sparring partner. All we do is fight. He makes me so mad. And I feel guilty afterwards. I feel so lonely." While I felt compassion, I also wondered whether Gail was trying to garner pity from the group.

"I don't pity you. You're a great-looking gal. You've made your bed, so you're sleeping in it." Mark got right to the point; tact was not his strongest suit.

"Look who's talking, Mark the marksman. How many women did you bed this week?" Annabel came to Gail's rescue and Mark piped down. Silence befell the group. Chad broke the silence.

"My mother's so stubborn. Her hearing's bad, but she won't listen to me. Why doesn't she wear her hearing aid? Instead, she complains bitterly that I don't speak loudly enough. She's driving me crazy. I don't want to hear her anymore; I just want her to shut up. Sometimes, I wish she'd shut up for good. Am I a horrible person?" Chad beseeched the group for mercy from his self-imposed prison of guilt.

"You're a good guy. You just feel too guilty. I also sometimes wish she'd die already. Then I ask myself, is it to relieve my pain or hers? That's when I feel I'm repulsive," Martha joined Chad.

"What I hear is guilt, guilt, and more guilt. And it's complicated. There's self-doubt, self-loathing, suffering, even self-pity, and feeling like a victim." I commented on the group's pain.

I suggested that the group take stock of their helping behaviors, so that they could objectively evaluate whether their guilt and shame were warranted. Making a written list of caring acts concretized the otherwise fuzzy perception of their worthiness, after which challenging their unjustified guilt was less arduous.

So what is it about guilt that makes it such a complex emotion? Stephen Mitchell outlined the distinctions between guilt, guiltiness (excessive guilt), and self-pity.[1] Regardless of whether or not hurtful actions are intentional, guilty feelings ensue. Guilt is hard to bear, so that defenses are employed to ward off painful feelings. One defense is excessive self-blame and suffering as though a mortal sin has been committed. It is a way of purchasing culpability in exchange for relief from pitiful helplessness.

Many, seeking exoneration and relief from pain, engage in cultural practices of penitent, unfelt gestures, and quick apologies. As children, we are taught to say "I'm sorry" very quickly. Politicians follow suit. Religion teaches us to repent from our sins and to seek speedy absolution. Rather than spend time thinking about why we failed, rituals are employed.

Another method is to blame others, as Sandra did. Self-pity and perceiving oneself as the victim are still other defenses against taking responsibility for one's role in destructive relationships.

Arduous, soul-searching, self-examination, and assumption of accountability are the road to true reparation. Guilty feelings that are not easily dismissed condition the soil for understanding. Love without understanding is hollow. In my practice, I come to love people after I understand their inner and outer worlds, as well as my feelings that are evoked by them. Compassion for your self is a loving embrace of goodness. The power of love paves the way for repair of guilty and unworthy feelings.[2]

Punitive feelings of guilt are the roadway to excessive self-sacrifice. Who really benefits from your martyrdom—your parents or you? When their autonomy is at stake, they feel patronized and diminished. Also, they may feel guilty taking so much from you, which they cannot repay.

Going beyond what is necessary does have a purpose. It serves to exonerate you from your suffering. There is another upshot from self-sacrifice. Overindulgence emits waves of resentment, with anger and self-pity riding the crest. Acting on these feelings brings more guilty feelings to the surface, as seen in Nancy's case.

Saints and Sinners

Raised with a Protestant work ethic and a Catholic conscience, Nancy kept house, worked as an advertising sales agent, raised the children, and meted out the discipline. As for her husband Ned, he played while she toiled. He was an irresponsible big kid. The children thought Dad was a blast. He also drank, did cocaine, and cheated on his wife. Nancy was his Madonna and the other women were his whores. He left clues around, which Nancy could not miss. Instead of confronting him, she suffered internally.

It took a lot for Nancy to lose it. One day, Nancy found Ned in bed with a tattooed, spike-haired, stoned bimbo. In a rage, Nancy threw them out of the house and filed for divorce. Then she suffered.

"You showed great strength in confronting him and divorcing him. I'd think you'd feel proud of yourself. Instead you're suffering," I noted.

"Somewhere, I think I failed him. More than that, I believe divorce is a sin and I'll go to hell." Nancy looked dejected and lifeless.

"So you're getting ready?" I played.

"I know it's stupid but I feel guilty, like a sinner." She was not playing with me.

"How convenient for Ned, he gets off the hook. You suffer his sins, like Jesus did for his people," I continued.

"Yeah, I'm good at that," Nancy sadly concurred.

"Now that your father's living with you, when do you have time to punish yourself? You're also a mother to three children, and you're working," I wondered.

"I don't really have time, but I find time. I feel depressed." For a brief moment while joining the game, her face brightened; then she grew somber.

"I can well imagine." I stayed with her.

"It's not just that I ended the marriage. That was bad enough. It's that I feel like I'm not doing the right thing with my father. He and I've been so close and now he needs me. He's weak and doesn't complain. I feel so sorry for him and I owe him so much. Don't get me wrong, I'm happy to care for him, it's just that I don't think I'm doing enough. I change him, make sure he eats, and I take time off from work to get him to his appointments. I can't be with him full time, so I hired outside nursing help. I have to work; we need the money. But I still feel guilty because I hired outside help." Nancy told me more of her story.

"Is the nursing help competent?" I inquired.

"Yes, very. It's just that Dad doesn't like her. I feel terrible, and . . ." Her voice trailed away as she moaned in pain.

"You have a long history of endurance, with your husband and now with your father." I commented on the ongoing process.

"I'm not always so patient with my father. This week I was on edge and I yelled at him. He did nothing wrong. The physical therapist said that he had enough muscle tone to sit up by himself and that I shouldn't help him. He argued that he couldn't do it. So, I tried to help him. I thought I was gentle, but he blamed me for handling him roughly and hurting his arm. God help me." Nancy raised her arms in prayer.

"How terrible." I commented on her dilemma.

"It gets better. Listen to this one. Would you believe when I let go, he sat up all by himself?" Nancy showed some verve, along with her anger.

"Maybe you're enfeebling your father with your over-the-top devotion. It may also be that you feel resentment and anger toward your dad. After all, your self-sacrificial role is meant for dead saints. You look quite alive." I smiled.

Nancy got the picture, and subsequent sessions revolved around her self-sacrificial role in the family. Her father, a hard-working landscaper, made just enough money to make ends meet for the family. As soon as the children were old enough, they worked at odd jobs to help out. Nancy, who was close to her father, sacrificed her playtime to work with him. When Nancy was ready to enter college, her mother took ill, so Nancy sacrificed her higher education for a care-taking role. After her mother died, Nancy married, which did not work out. So she endured a great many hardships. Her father's illness was the culminating one; fearing his loss, she went overboard in caring for him.

Getting in touch with her unconscious wish to keep him alive at all costs to her, coupled with her habitual role as the sufferer, awakened a maelstrom of conflicting emotions. In therapy, we worked through many of these contradictory needs and wishes. At midlife, watching her father die, Nancy arrived at the realization that she only had a finite time to live. Indeed, her wish to live for him conflicted with her desire to live for herself.

Seeing how her well-intentioned overprotection backfired, only to enfeeble her father further, was an eye opener. This insight helped Nancy reach for healthier options. Her split-off need for pleasure, which she had associated with sinning, took on new meaning. She finally decided it was her turn to reap some of the benefits of her years of hard work. She has engaged in some pleasurable activity and her father seems to respect her more.

Parents may project guilt onto you. They may feel guilty or self-pity because they did not live their lives fully and richly. Instead they scrimped and saved to provide you with the best. To top it off, they made sure to let you know about their sacrifices. So, you feel guilty when it comes to caring for your self.

Some people ingest mandates from parents to please other people, to fit in, to conform as ways to secure love and curry favor. Spitting out these orders and doing as one pleases arouses guilt pangs.

I have noticed that depressed parents often have a way of inducing guilty feelings. Anger that is turned inward is related to depression. I have seen where anger is so plentiful it turns inward and also spills outward. Raging parents may accuse you of doing terrible things. Their fury serves two purposes: momentary relief from depression and absolution of their guilt. Scurrying around in your mind in search of your transgressions, you take on the guilt. Hence the tables are turned. You are the suffering victim, and your parent has won a Pyrrhic victory.

WHERE DID YOU LEARN TO SUFFER?

I do not know about you, but I learned to suffer from my Jewish mother. But you do not have to be Jewish to suffer unduly. In my practice, I work with sufferers in all shades of ethnicity, race, and religion. Suffering is right up there with saintliness. Saints, however, are in heaven. Long-suffering souls live a hell here on earth.

Intergenerational transmission of values and belief systems is partly how we develop. People who worry and torture themselves over issues that are out of their control have parents and grandparents who have done the same. They have internalized their parents' ways.

Great works of literature are filled with tragedy and suffering, from William Shakespeare to Elie Weisel. Many works speak to the ability of humans to forge rich lives from the ashes of misfortune. People flock to

Broadway plays where characters are beset with misfortune. *Les Miserables* and *La Boheme* are musical productions about human tragedy. Toulouse-Lautrec's depiction of the gaiety of Parisian nightlife is more poignant because of his personal story of suffering. On the other hand, Pablo Picasso led a free-wheeling life and many of his paintings reflected such. Nevertheless, Picasso empathized with the horrors of the Spanish Civil war in his famous painting, *Guernica*. To appreciate these works, we identify with the pathos.

Misery has still other origins. We may learn how to treat ourselves by internalizing and identifying with how parents treated us.[3] Hence, if parents were excessive in their punishment, we begin to punish ourselves. They have written the script, and their voices remain in our heads. Maybe it is time to rewrite the script.

Suffering does not have to be self-punitive. It may strengthen one to arrive at a deeper, richer level of existence. To bear painful scars is an integral aspect of human experience. When is suffering desirable and when is it debilitating? It depends. The key is partly how long the pain continues to disarm you, and how you resolve it. Prolonged suffering of old scars utilizes a lot of energy, which may be put to better use. A better option is to transform the pain to robust, productive living and loving. That option entails energy that invigorates rather than enervates. Let us look at long-suffering Linda in the following case study.

Loveless Linda

When I met Linda, she was broken and bent. The dark winter sky matched her mood. Her face was swollen from crying, her hair tangled, and her clothes disheveled. Her gaze was turned sideways out the window, where bare trees were silhouetted against the bleak winter sky. She avoided eye contact with me, as she sobbed tears of sorrow.

Her story was replete with trauma, abuse, and suffering in her childhood at the hands of her parents. In her marriage, she suffered from domestic violence perpetrated by her husband. He divorced her four years ago and Linda was devastated without him. She could not get him out of her mind. Nightmares and flashbacks intruded her sleep and waking hours. She reported intrusive thoughts, depression, anxiety, and panic attacks. Linda did not stop there; she mutilated herself and attempted suicide several times before we met. Her suffering had no limits.

Her father was feeble and close to death. Her parents were divorced and her mother lived in another city. Despite the childhood abuse, Linda felt obligated to care for him. She was burdened beyond her capacity.

"I don't know what I did to deserve such a life," she despaired.

"What do you think?" I inquired.

"I think I've been a good person. So, why am I suffering so much?" Linda pleaded with me.

"Well, you've spoken a lot about how punitive your parents were to you in childhood. Then you married a man like your parents, who continued where they left off. You've told me how much you miss Andrew, your abusive ex-husband. So, what do you miss? His abuse?" I was baffled.

"God, no. I don't miss that." Linda continued to weep.

"Actually you don't have to miss his abuse; you've made up for it. You abuse yourself. Now that Andrew and your parents are out of the picture, you have no one to torture you. So you torture yourself with traumatic memories, cutting yourself and overdosing on pills." I stabbed at her and caught myself feeling guilty at my aggressive approach.

"You're tough, like my father." Linda stopped crying, sat up straight, looked me in the eye and fired back. "You remind me of him. He blamed me for everything and didn't believe me. You don't believe me." She actually looked feisty as she defended herself.

"With your history, I don't blame you for feeling that I attacked you. There's a huge difference, however, between blaming and holding yourself responsible for your actions. You're addicted to suffering; we have to find a better way. I believe we can work together to re-create a healthier woman. You've told me about your rewarding singing career that was shelved. Maybe you could dust it off and start singing again. If I remember correctly, you sing jazz and the blues."

Together, we worked on transforming the ashes of Linda's tragic life to a life with meaning. She began to see that she treated herself as her prior abusers had. Her father's death was a pivotal time for her, and she thought it was time to make some changes. Slowly, her suffering abated and her horizons brightened. Spring was finally here.

PLEASURE WITHOUT PAIN

> Every child is an artist. The problem is
> to remain an artist once he grows up.
> Pablo Picasso

Playing and Boundaries

Can you experience pleasure unfettered by the pain of guilt? Can you give yourself permission to play, engage in fun experiences, and enjoy relationships? Can you set limits? Plagued by "shoulds," your punitive superego is working overtime and prevents you from setting limits for your parents or yourself.

Taking pleasure leaves some people feeling guilty as though they are betraying parents. Others feel shame about betraying an idealized image of themselves as all-giving, kind, and loving people. They have no boundaries around themselves. I am not suggesting rigid boundaries that leave no room for interaction with others. I am talking about permeable boundaries. The term *boundary* implies setting some limits to you as a separate person, with separate needs and desires. The term *permeable* suggests a flexible boundary that allows for intimate interaction. So, it is a way you may care for your parents while caring for you.

Play is a healthy distraction to combat burnout. A break revitalizes inner resources. By the way, you are not the only one to benefit. Your parents stand to gain when you feel refreshed and energized. I always find that taking a break helps me to see things in a more clear light. Carefree fun allows for more thoughtful caring. Heavy feelings of burden, stress, emotional turmoil, guilt, and shame exhaust us, and loving care is compromised. A lighter heart goes a long way.

Sex and Play

How about sex? If you think sex is overindulgent play, I would suggest you think again. Sex with a loving partner is not only a form of pleasure, it is also a form of comfort. And comfort is sorely needed when you are easing the discomforts of aging parents. While feelings of guilt and unworthiness hover overhead, your body hungers for pleasure and sexual gratification. Sex with a responsive partner feeds our bodies, minds and our souls. Sexual satisfaction brings feelings of gratitude, tenderness, and increased love.[2] Hence, feelings of guilt and unworthiness are countervailed and replaced with feelings of security, appreciation, and greater psychological health. Positive feelings and mood carry over to how you experience and care for your parents. Sally's reclaiming of her sexuality in the following story illustrates some of these points.

Sullied Sally

Sally lived alone for many years after her divorce. Her elderly mother was now failing. She feared her mother's death for many reasons. One reason was that Sally would be the oldest remaining family member. The brevity of her life signaled her need to make the most of the remaining years. She decided to combat her loneliness and find a man. An intelligent, attractive, and worldly woman, Sally had a lot to offer. Her quest was short, and Sally was soon involved with a man.

Mario made her laugh. He was a poet who wrote limericks and taught Italian at a university. Sally was an economics professor at the same university. Their personalities complemented each other. Mario was carefree and spontaneous, whereas Sally was cautious and less flexible. They both liked fun and took pleasure in common interests.

Sally wished to keep their romance discreet. She explained that gossip was prevalent amongst the faculty, and she did not want to give them fodder to feed on. Mario flirted outrageously with Sally in front of the faculty. Sally, a seasoned worrywart, had something new to fret about.

"What'll they think of me?" Consternation showed in Sally's tightened posture.

"What're you concerned about?" I asked.

"I know I shouldn't, but I care about what people think of me. I'm making a fool of myself. The faculty knows that my mother's very sick and that I'm screwing around with Mario. I feel sullied." Sally lowered her eyes. " It's not only what they think; it's also what I think. Sex outside of marriage is a sin that I knowingly commit." Her eyes were glued to the floor.

"So, you feel shame and guilt. Do you enjoy sex with Mario?" I delved further.

"That's the problem. Sex is wonderful. He's an attentive, sensitive lover." Sally was smitten.

"Why's this pleasure such a problem?" I continued to probe.

"How can I have fun and sexual pleasure when she's so feeble and miserable? I feel disloyal to her. I feel that what I'm doing's wrong; it's immoral." The lovesick look was replaced with a chagrined little-girl look.

Sally's harsh critical superego got in the way of her pleasure and, as we discovered, in the way of caring for her ill mother. She found herself resenting her mother and trying to avoid her. Actually, Sally was running away from her own crushing feelings.

When Sally finally came to terms with her emotions, she felt better about caring for her mother. She also found that sex and play with Mario lifted her sagging spirits so that she was more available and responsive to her mother.

Caring for Your Self

He enjoys true leisure who has time
to improve his soul's estate.

Henry David Thoreau

I cannot emphasize enough the importance of self-care. As a therapist, I am unable to adequately care for the emotional needs of my patients unless I care for my own emotional needs. I would not be equipped to think, create, or write if I was not able to suspend reason, fantasize, and play at times. As a middle-generation child, obligations may rend you apart with self-doubts and guilt. Forgetting your self, when dealing with elderly, ill parents, is so easy. In a comprehensive study, nearly all the caregivers had no time for leisure.[1]

In transitional times of trauma and stress, we feel fragmented and unstable—not like our selves. At least not like the person we have come to know as "me." Feeling like a stranger in your own skin does not bode well for your parents' psychological health or yours. Focusing on your self helps to pull you together to relate in a more vital, cohesive manner.

The more you care for your parents and the less you care for your self, the more depleted you feel and the less they benefit; this is another example of a zero-sum game. With a paucity of inner resources, you draw on less than desirable, possibly unhealthy remedies. Rather than relishing the remaining hours with your elderly parents, you feel repulsed by them. With inner worlds devoid of nutrition, you are unable to nurture others; nurturing and caring begin at home. An enriched personal life helps to bolster you for this intense process.

SELF-CARE

> Self-love, my liege, is not so vile a sin,
> as self-neglecting.
>
> William Shakespeare

Self-care implies self-love. Self-love has gotten a bad rap and is confused with self-involvement, conceit, and a swelled head—narcissism. Actually self-love may be a good thing. Self-absorption negates relating to others with love. What is more, obsessive narcissism may be downright dangerous. Narcissus drowned in the pool of his own reflection because he was so self-absorbed. For Freud, narcissism was pathological and infantile. He believed that narcissistic patients were so far gone that they could not be analyzed.

A shift in attitudes finds that contemporary analytic thinkers[2,3] value narcissism as a healthy aspect of mature behavior. We now refer to narcissism as high self-esteem, which inspires expression of the self. Artists and writers utilize their narcissism to create, to impart information, and to convey the aesthetic. Healthy narcissism facilitates aspirations and goals. Teachers with healthy narcissism help to develop young minds.

People with high self-esteem are firmly planted internally. They can bend without the fear of breaking. Their flexibility permits them to be broadminded and open to opinions and attitudes that differ from their own. Conversely, people with low self-esteem feel shaky and fear losing their fragile identity by otherness. Often the compensation is arrogant behavior and rigidity. Sean is a case in point.

Rogues to Riches

Sean's quest for adoration had no bounds. While Sean may be described as narcissistic, he was also a complex, fascinating blend of qualities. Well developed in intellectual, critical thought, Sean also had street smarts. His arrogant, domineering manner would give way to charm and flirtation. At times, I found him entertaining, and at other times, irksome.

As a child, Sean's father was physically abusive toward him. His mother betrayed little Sean by siding with her husband. Sean was haunted by memories of the beatings, his smallness, and his sense of powerlessness. As an adolescent, Sean found relief from emotional pain in drugs, which soon became his escape from his self. Before long, he was dealing in drugs, making big money, sporting showy women and fancy cars. Everything came to an abrupt stop when he was incarcerated. Despite humiliation in jail, Sean used his cunning to get by and survived intact. Out on the street again, he repeated his cycle of rise and fall ten times.

Two years prior to entering therapy, Sean met a wealthy widow and married her. Overnight he climbed from rogues to riches. They traveled first class and he felt like a king. Sean's trip to Tahiti was cut short when his sister summoned him home. His mother was dying. Sean had mixed feelings about his mother and spent time sorting them out.

In therapy, our dialogue was disconcerting. Sean did not communicate with me. He lectured to me and expected me to sit in awe. He was well versed in worldly matters, history, and economics. Not so, in matters of his heart. Sean artfully dodged me when I tried to address his emotional life or his relationships.

"How do you like my jacket? It's an Armani, so are the pants." Sean made sure that I did not miss his designer clothes.

"Looks good on you. You're a good dresser," I responded candidly.

"Thanks; you look good, too, Doc. Blue's a good color on you." He complimented my appearance.

"I know you're going to tell me I'm avoiding my self. So here goes. That group leader that I told you about, Dr. Shane, the one who's leading the aging parents support group, well, she's whacked. She said I was out of line. All I did was give this guy some advice. His mother's got stomach cancer like my mother. I know a lot about the subject. More than the leader, that's for sure." Sean was condescending to the group leader, as he'd been to me in many sessions.

"You seem to resent the leader," I commented.

"I don't resent her. What's your problem?" Sean was furious.

"What do you feel now?" I wanted him to address his feelings.

"I feel nothing. That Shane babe, she's not worth me feeling anything." Sean blew me off and held the group leader in contempt. In doing so, he appointed himself the supreme judge of worthiness.

"Maybe she could perceive what you think about her?" I kept trying to bring Sean to some place of self-awareness.

"No way, I'm good at faking people out." He just about pounded his chest.

"I see." I smiled. I saw more than he wanted me to.

"What do you mean by that? You're attacking me, just like the group leader." There came the narcissistic blow, his paranoia and counterattack.

"So, if I hold an opinion that differs from yours, you feel attacked. If I were in total accord with you, how would you feel?" I continued.

"Great." Sean was candid.

"With your background of attack by parents, your sensitivity to others who differ from you is understandable," I interpreted.

Outwardly, Sean was full of himself. Inside he was empty. Disavowing his feelings of weakness and shame, he constructed a compensatory ideal self as all-powerful. The ideal self was a sham—a false self. Sean was not open to other people's opinions, as they may have dislodged his shaky identity built on a flimsy foundation, decorated with tinsel. He flaunted his intelligence and his attire, seeking approval. Quick to bruise, he nevertheless had no compunctions about insulting others.

In therapy, Sean came to see how disavowal of his feelings of power-lessness and shame were being enacted in arrogant, pushy ways. Instead of impressing people and garnering favor, he was turning them off. What is more, his paranoia and style of blaming others was his way of guarding his fragile self-esteem. That did not work for him either; projecting his rage on to others (his wish to attack me was distorted as my wish to attack him) left him feeling evacuated. And he was at others' mercy to change, which is highly unlikely. The only one he could change was his self, not others. That realization, in part, helped him to feel more hopeful and powerful.

Re-creating Sean's view of his self, based on his considerable strengths, revealed a healthy wish to help others. He had completed his doctoral studies in public health and was in the process of doing his dissertation, known in the field as ABD (all but the dissertation). Actually, he had been struggling with a thesis for the last five years. Finally, he found a topic and decided to compare the socioeconomic and psychological effects of HIV disease with hepatitis C disease. His mentors were encouraging, and Sean plowed into the work with zealous fervor. Constant critique by his reviewers was difficult for him to tolerate. Initially, criticism smarted, but in short time, Sean was able to separate his father's destructive abuse from the reviewers' constructive comments. Also, he kept the larger picture in mind. He would help a lot of underprivileged people and expose prejudice. Is that fulfilling a narcissistic wish? Indeed it is; this healthy narcissism is an integral part of writers, artists, politicians, researchers, and many other people who make wonderful contributions to society.

His mother's death brought Sean to therapy. His intelligence and curiosity helped, and he became enamored with the process of insight. Psychoanalysis is a journey into the soul of the patient, and Sean loved the focus on him. In time, he was able to feel stronger internally, to help others, and to be more considerate of others feelings.

SELF-SOOTHING

The ability to soothe one's self is a basic function that is internalized in early childhood. Parents in attunement with infants are responsive to signs of hunger, distress, or discomfort. Not everyone has experienced that early Eden-like interaction. And even if you have, it would still be nice to have a parent to soothe you. Unfortunately, you must do the soothing now.

People with healthy self-esteem are flexible and they dissociate, knowing full well that they will return to a sense of unity and of identity as "me." Dissociation in service of the self revives you; it is a mark of strength and not pathology. Dissociation, or distraction from worry and duty, benefits caregivers. So, why not draw on your flexible side and consider the need for relief from worry, distress, and duty? Distracting your self replenishes you so that stress is eased.

Review of successful self-soothing practices in prior crises is helpful. See what worked in the past and adapt it to your present circumstances. Then there is humor. Seeing the irony of things and chuckling at your self is great fun. There is nothing like a good laugh. Comedic movies, TV shows, and joke books evoke mirth and mitigate stress.

I encourage you to find time for emotional and physical health. Sports, walks, working out, gardening, or other outdoor activities refurbish spirits. Healthy nutrition and a sensible diet provide energy. Caring for your hair, nails, and skin gives a lift. One of my patients told me she would not leave her mother at home alone; she decided to take her mother along with her to the beauty parlor. Another man taught his father to do crossword puzzles to keep him occupied while he attended to his own needs. Still another man, who wanted to watch a TV show with his wife, gently directed his mother to the TV in the kitchen. He made sure his mother's favorite snack was on the kitchen table.

Time out from responsibilities for carefree, even aimless activity is not a no-no. You may need it. Crashing on the sofa, watching an entertaining TV show, even if it is trashy, gives you the respite you need. Listening to soothing music, playing with pets, and talking to friends are healing activities.

SUPPORT SYSTEMS

On-line support groups, group therapy, friends, and family members are resources to help you manage. The benefits of emotional support are well documented. Researchers demonstrated that women who juggled diverse role demands benefited from emotional support. They had less anxiety, strain, and depression.[4,5,6]

Midlife women caring for impaired parents who received emotional support from husbands, children, or co-workers felt a greater sense of mastery in that role and greater psychological fitness. They also had a greater feeling of well-being, with less depression and more life satisfaction.[7] Emotional support consisted of partners listening to concerns and feelings, showing respect and thoughtful behaviors, and

Problems from the Past

Life can only be understood backwards;
but must be lived forwards.

Soren Kierkegaard

Neurotics build castles in the air,
psychotics live in them.
My mother cleans them.

Rita Rudner

Old ghosts that have lain dormant are now haunting. Unresolved problems from childhood, long buried, resurface. There is pressure to resolve these issues before parents die, which may be a good thing or a bad thing. Resurgence of anxiety, depression, or anger comes with the territory.

Painful experiences make life's journey more difficult, but they also enrich and deepen personality. Given the urgency imposed by the truncated time span, the need to rise from the ashes of bottomless suffering to the apex of self-discovery is greater than ever.

Examining the past, we come across pieces of the puzzle. Prior interactions influence our relationship to our selves and to others. Loving, happy relationships increase trust and hopeful attitudes; they provide a firm foundation during stressful times. Overindulgence decreases ability to tolerate frustration and accept rejection, which may present problems now. Other issues that may loom large are histories of neglect, criticism, or abandonment.

Holding on to the hurtful past and longterm suffering arrests creative living. You have choices to make. You can remain mired in misery or you can say "enough." At midlife, time is of the essence. The challenge lies in extricating your self from the morass of strangling emotions for a freer tomorrow.

CHILDHOOD ISSUES REVISITED

Old feelings and unfulfilled wishes are rekindled. Distant disappointments, anger, and sadness emerge mercilessly during this process. Some adult children maintain dichotomous perceptions of their parents as saint/sinner, all good/bad, or idealized/demonized. The advent of aging and death worsens these splits. Once you see parents in a more realistic light and as more whole people, you can better accept the good and bad parts of both them and you. In that way, you gain a greater feeling of internal strength to keep you balanced. The world need not turn all black when things go wrong; bear in mind the bright sides. Doug's case illustrates the resurgence of problems from the past.

Dominic the Demonic

Doug was a sad, frustrated, angry man. Casually dressed in jeans and a sweatshirt, his body was lean and muscular. His stride was usually sprightly so that his persona assumed the appearance of youthful vitality. Lately, he had a hangdog look about him. His walk was devoid of vigor and his entire being had lost its luster.

"I feel like an old man, like I'm falling apart. I can't get myself to play a game of tennis or to run like I used to. I feel so guilty about my mother that I can't do anything but worry about her. I can't eat or sleep," Doug sulked.

"I know you've been a dedicated son, so why the guilt?" I asked.

It was his father, Dominic. "He's taken over her care. I don't know what to do," Doug complained.

"Why's that such a problem?" I wondered.

"He does more harm than good. He insulted the doctor, the nurses, the entire hospital, just like he's always insulted me. He yelled at the doctor, that he didn't know what he was doing, that he was an asshole. Then he called the nurse a fat cow. He insists on caring and making decisions for my weak, dying mother. That's a joke; she took care of him his whole life. He can't even boil water for himself." Doug was furious.

"What does your mother say?" I was curious about that.

"She's out of it, so she doesn't know what's happening. She goes along with my father. My wife thinks it's none of my business, that my father's her husband. Now he's suddenly her husband? He never did anything for her before this. I was always there for my mother and she was there for me. How can I desert her now?" he cried out.

"It sounds like you and your mother had a special relationship. Almost like you were her husband," I interpreted.

"My father was always jealous of our close relationship. He undermined me and that's what he's doing now." He continued to talk about his father, not himself.

"So, this is a case of good cop, bad cop," I noted.

"My mother's always been an angel and my father's the devil himself." He confirmed my interpretation.

Doug had unresolved lifelong issues with his domineering, critical father. The Oedipal triangle, not fully resolved, was temporarily buried when he married and had children. Suddenly, it reared its head. Doug feared losing his mother, whereas his father feared the same fate. They were both still fighting for her affections.

His beloved mother was near death. Doug thought only he could make the right decisions about her medical and nursing care. His father, firmly believing in his own capabilities, dismissed Doug. The battle with his father intensified as they competed to help his mother. Doug felt he was fighting a losing battle. Unfortunately, his mother was the one to lose out. Her deterioration and painful demise were intensified by Doug's guilt and anger toward his father.

Doug was faced with the daunting challenge of examining his past. His mother's relationship with her irascible husband was strained, whereas her relationship with her mild-mannered son Doug was warm and close. Indeed, as Doug explained, his father was jealous of the mother-son affections. In early childhood, perceiving his father as his rival for his mother's affections, Doug was enraged with him. Unconscious guilt about his hateful feelings for his father conflicted with his wish to have him disappear from his life.

He perceived his mother Eva as the angelic one and his father Dominic as the demonic one. He told me that his wife thought that he was more like his father. In therapy, Doug either criticized everything about his wife or he praised her. His feelings about her went from good to bad overnight, as they did about me. I fell into the role of the accepting, caring therapist or the prickly, attacking one. Often, our vivid interactions resulted in heated debate.

Coming to terms with his conflict about his father and his futile wish for his mother were issues that were laid on the table. Focus on his marriage, with ways to satisfy his wife and revive warm feelings, emerged as a centerpiece. Doug was able to relinquish his unconscious wish for his mother and to work out his Oedipal conflict partly by making room for his wife's nurturance. A more realistic perception of his mother coupled with his wife's love was most healing in his time of sorrow.

The earlier tasks of separation-individuation are revisited during the care-taking process.[1] Adult children often regress to an earlier stage of development, and former feelings and behaviors are reawakened. Although adult children may be living independent lives, separation issues thought to be resolved emerge once again, as in Anita's story.

Anita in Need

Anita, with her tied-back hair, slim, tailored pants, and stalwart build, was poised for action. A social worker with a mission in life, Anita wished to help others less fortunate than her. She was protective of her clients, fought the system, and acted as an advocate for the poor. As a child, her mother worked hard and ran the household with an iron fist. Her father was a softie and deftly ducked his wife.

A high-spirited, independent-minded child, Anita defied her mother's rules. She shouted back at her mother and her mother beat her. No matter the sting of the beatings, Anita stubbornly remained sullen and dry eyed, giving her a sense of superior power and independence. Mayhem was the order, or rather disorder, of the day. Her father stayed out of the fray, retreated to his room, and claimed migraine headaches. Anita had mixed feelings about her mother. She admired her strengths, but she despised her harshness. Her feelings about her father were unequivocal. He was everything wonderful, a talented architect, artist, avid reader—a Renaissance man.

In therapy, she discovered that she resented her father's weakness and pined for a more protective father figure. At her job, she identified with her mother's role as the strong one, and her wished-for father's role as the protective one. What is more, she vicariously identified with a disavowed part of her self that she found with her dependent, needy clients. She married a quiet intellectual man, who in some ways reminded her of her father.

Her mother had died two years earlier, and now her aging father was suffering from heart disease. Anita was devastated at the sight of her father's shrinking body and his neediness; old separation issues arose. Her wish for a strong protective father was at odds with the reality of the situation; her weak father needed her to care for him.

"I was independent; I moved out of the house and moved on with my life. Now I feel like a baby again. I'm crying like a big baby. I actually came down with a nasty sore throat and I needed my husband to care for me. That's not like me. I'm ashamed of my neediness. Please help me." Anita let her hair down and sobbed. She entreated me to collude with her rescue fantasies.

"I'll try." I was tempted to save her.

"I dreamed last night that a monster was chasing a little girl. The child was running barefoot, with only a diaper on. Then she was in a lake, with the water coming up over her head. She almost drowned, when a boy came to her rescue. He fought with the monster and killed him. That's when I woke up." Anita presented me with a gift. A dream to an analyst is precious for its interpretive value. Freud called a dream the royal road to the unconscious.

"It appears that you feel endangered by your old demons. Could be your mother's aggression or your wish to be taken care of. Although your needs are normal, you've disowned them. You feel you're drowning and wish to be rescued." I tried to repay her generosity with insight.

"Yeah I feel like I'm drowning and wish my father was able to save me," she associated to my interpretation.

"The theme of this dream is searching for a protective father figure. A lot of adult children feel they're regressing to earlier stages. I also notice that you want me to rescue you, to protect you from your painful feelings. By the way, why are you so ashamed of your neediness?" I inquired.

"I'm an adult and I'm acting like a baby. I wish my father would be able to cradle me, to comfort me. I'm ashamed of needing him, when he's the one who's really in need." Anita wept openly and reached for the tissues. I moved the tissue box closer to her.

Anita and I worked on resolving her conflict surrounding dependency needs: her wish to be cared for conflicted with her wish to be independent and separate. She toyed with the idea of relying on her husband, only to fear engulfment and a loss of her self. The alternative was loneliness and pseudo-independence, based on fear and not internal strength. Finally, she decided to test her neediness with her husband. In time she found that she could be an independent person with needs for protection, and that she could lean on her husband, just as he could on her. As a separate independent woman in an interdependent relationship, Anita felt more whole.

NOW OR NEVER

Histories of rejection, alienation, or friction in childhood are related to adult children's unwillingness to care for elderly parents. Adult children are often in conflict about their unkind feelings on one hand and their feelings of love, attachment, obligation, or duty on the other hand.

Discordant feelings are distressful. To ease our discomfort, we may either act precipitously or avoid situations. Overwhelming feelings obfuscate the issue of controlling feelings and thinking rationally, and objectivity about making decisions is compromised. Hence, discerning when to let parents maintain autonomy that would be helpful to them, when to intervene, or when to ask for outside help is clouded.[1]

Many of us feel that it is now or never—that time to resolve longstanding issues is running out. It is hard to accept that if these issues have not been resolved until now, the likelihood that they would be resolved now is low.

LETTING GO

A term that is bandied about lightly is *letting go*. Letting go, however, is not a frivolous or simple act. It is a serious and complex process. In time, there is relief, but first there is some difficult work. Mourning the concrete reality of death is hard enough. Mourning intangible, firmly held illusions or fantasies is even harder. Loss of either a loved one or a cherished hope is painful. Sometimes the two losses merge, and the pain of mourning the death of parents is intensified by our unmet wishes.

The wish that parents will gratify you and change before they die is a futile fantasy. Relinquishing the wish for a state of bliss and unity with parents is sad. Since we began life in the womb in a state of union with parents, many of us hold on to that primitive wish for oceanic bliss. Now, however, the sad reality is that the tomb looms large. So, letting go is a melancholy business.

Mourning also entails the sad process of relinquishing the illusion of parents as providers and security figures. The danger in not sufficiently mourning the illusion of parents as omnipotent rescuers lies in your propensity to search out other people to save you. Indeed, there are many people with rescue fantasies whom you may meet. Or you may unwittingly elicit rescue behavior from them. Rather than moving on with your life, you remain stagnant with feelings of dependency and melancholy to which you are accustomed. Mourning the old and familiar is essential before embarking on a new stage of life.[1] Pamela, in the following story, is a case in point.

Persistent Pamela

A charming, accomplished concert pianist, Pamela was humble about her talents. She attributed her success to her diligence. It took a lot of practice and sacrifice in childhood to get where she wanted. She played with famous conductors and orchestras internationally. Arthritis threatened to cripple her, but she did not give up. Pamela summoned her willpower and got some relief from anti-inflammatory medication, massage, and finger exercises. Also, she developed a high tolerance for endurance, so she withstood the pain and continued to play beautiful music.

"I'm fortunate enough to play wonderful works of great masters, but I can't get the relationship with my mother to work." Pamela was frustrated.

"She's the master you can't seem to master," I joked, but was dead serious. Although she wished to master her mother, her mother resisted.

"Yeah, I can play beautiful music in perfect harmony with others, but not with my mother." Pamela was in concert with me.

"So, you want her to be in accord with you. Instead you have discord," I reflected.

"I've been trying to get her to notice me since I was a child. Let me show you this picture." She pulled out an old, faded picture.

"Cute baby. She seemed to have been absorbed in you then," I noted.

"That's not me she's holding. It's my brother. This was my third birthday party and I'm shoved in back. My sister and my other brothers were bigger than me, so they hid me. You can hardly see me," Pamela was distressed.

"And you feel she can hardly see you now," I interpreted.

"She called me yesterday to complain about the pain in her hip. She has arthritis. I guess that's where I got it. So, I asked her if she took her medicine. She couldn't remember and kept me on the phone for an hour grumbling about her aches, her lousy doctors, her selfish children, and how alone she felt. She knew I was home alone with bronchitis. I kept coughing, so she couldn't help but notice. She didn't notice. It was all about her," Pamela complained bitterly.

"So you still want her to attend to you, but she's self-absorbed." I merged with her.

"I asked her 'what do you want from me?' How should I know whether she took her medicine or not?" She repeated the provocative dialogue.

"Huh!" I joined her.

"She ignored me and just continued with her long-winded stories. When I talk she doesn't hear me; she's in her own head." Pamela was enraged.

"How awful for you," I commented.

"On Mother's Day, I took her to lunch at a lovely restaurant. She complained that the food was too spicy. I told her to tell the waiter, not me. I'm also a mother, but she didn't once say 'happy Mother's Day' to me," she lamented.

"So, you want her to acknowledge and appreciate you. How old is your mother now?" I asked.

"She's eighty-nine," Pamela responded.

"I've got to give it to you. You're persistent." I got to the point.

"What for? She's never going to change." Pamela looked sad, very sad.

"Indeed. You've come to a sad, sobering conclusion. As sad as it is, it'll help you go on with your life. You seem stuck in your love life. Seymour was attentive at first; then his true self came out. He was self-absorbed and self-centered. You kept hoping he'd change, but he didn't either. Then there was Alan, who was stuck on you, and you soon found that you had competition. He was really stuck on himself. I think John was hot tempered, not so hot in bed, and unavailable when you needed him. He wanted you when he wanted you. You repeat the same pattern," I confronted her.

"I'm persistent, all right. Persistent Pamela, that's me." She chuckled bravely, with tears close by.

"So, maybe it's time to mourn the illusion that your mother will change. Maybe you're finding new mothers in these men and you keep hoping they'll change. When they don't, you're disappointed. We can't rely on others to change; it only leaves us at their mercy. That scenario's scary. Taking initiative for our lives augers for a healthier outcome." I tried to offer her some hope.

Mourning the illusion that one day her mother would acknowledge her was long and arduous. But once again, Pamela rose to the challenge and persisted to let go of her futile wish. After a short while, she noticed a fellow pianist who did admire and attend to her. A talented and generous woman, there was much to admire. As the relationship developed, Pamela continued to find him affirming and loving, as she was of him. And together, they played beautiful music.

CHANGES AS ADULT CHILDREN

The only one who can change is you—the adult child. Learning to avoid the pitfalls of repeating old, familiar, but faulty interactions with new people is one way to change. That involves seeing how you may unconsciously find people with similar characteristics to your parents. It also means recognizing how you may provoke others into patterns of relating that are similar to childhood interactions.

An important concept in contemporary psychoanalysis is known as *internal object relations*. This theory refers to the way childhood relationships and experiences become internalized as durable features. We then anticipate that in our daily encounters with adult reality, we will run into the same characters and events.[2,3] Old, familiar scenes are comfortable, so we find new players to play out the old dramas. Pamela persisted in her role with her mother and found new players in the men in her life.

To transform ourselves, we must take a good hard look at ourselves, the good, the bad, and the ugly. In marital therapy, couples are intent on blaming and faulting their partners. Each partner wishes the other one would change. Facing one's own shortcomings is hard; pointing the finger is easier. Interactions change when partners engage in self-examination of cherished, as well as dreaded qualities. Empathy for the other is not far off. So, this may be an opportunity to bring the mirror up close, examine warts and winning traits, and begin the transformation process.

Unfinished Family Business

The shoe that fits one person pinches another;
there is no recipe for living that suits all cases.
Carl Jung

Unfinished business with siblings is on the table. Conflicts stemming from old rivalries make this time even more stressful. Aging parents, weak, ill, and often demented, are unable to make sound decisions. Relatives are resources. Who takes responsibility and makes the tough decisions? Is the caregiver undermined or supported? What factors determine who provides the bulk of care? Can conflicts be set aside and responsibilities shared? Does providing care for elderly parents have to be equal?

In a recent meta-analysis, authors integrated the findings of eighty-four studies.[1] They found caregivers reported more symptoms than noncaregivers. The differences between the two groups were in depression, subjective feelings of wellness, physical health, and effectiveness. Although differences were significant, they were moderate to small. The largest effect was depression. Also, larger differences were found in dementia caregivers than other caregivers. The authors speculated as to the relatively small differences. One possible reason was that caregivers received stress-buffering support. Another possibility was the positive aspects of providing care, such as feeling useful. Understanding the meanings of the provision of care is complex. In addition to strain and tensions, providing care leads to satisfaction.[2]

Researchers showed that siblings caring for elderly parents coordinated their efforts in half the families, and provided partial help in one fourth. In these families, each sibling helped with care as he or she wished. In still another fourth, siblings provided no help at all.[3] Another study corroborated the findings that there was no norm; the range of participation and cooperation varied widely.[4] In most cases one sibling provided the bulk of care and conflict among siblings abounded. Resentment toward siblings who did not participate was felt by three fourths of siblings who volunteered.[2]

Family history was the underlying chief factor that affected who would help and the ensuing conflict.[4] With a history of satisfying relationships with parents, adult children were more apt to volunteer to provide care. For these siblings, the close childhood tie got even closer in adulthood. In turn, prior conflict with parents was related to unwillingness to participate in providing care.

Obvious issues that influence provision of care are geographical proximity, work, and family commitments.[4] Aside from geographical proximity, which is a central factor in who provides care, there is the issue of timing of life's events.[5]

Hence, if siblings are already caring for ailing spouses or disturbed adolescent children, they are less prone to help with elderly parents. That scenario is more apparent and understandable to siblings who take on the responsibility. More problematic and less obvious are old parent-child emotional problems that have left adult children with bitterness and unwillingness to help. Resentful siblings who assume the brunt of the work are not always able to comprehend siblings' feelings, let alone be sympathetic to them.

Gender was yet another factor that determined who took on the caretaker role, with significantly more women than men doing so.[6] The emotional bond between mothers and daughters was the strongest motivating factor in why daughters assumed the burden. Some women simply took on the traditional role of mother as the nurturer, homemaker, and caregiver. Another factor was that women outlived men by ten years. As a result of greater longevity, more women were available as caregivers.

In another study, some adult children thought they should not assume the role, as other siblings were more fit. Sons believed daughters were more fit. And daughters-in-law thought daughters were more fit.[2] Within the pecking order, once again, more women took on the caretaker role. If children felt abandoned by parents or experienced divorce or custody issues, they were less apt to offer help.[4] In other cases, volunteers refused help when offered. Sole care of parents served to make these siblings feel more powerful and morally superior.

COMPETITION

Old rivalries prevent cooperation. Competing for parents' approval hinders the sharing of responsibilities. Rivalry stemming from early childhood frustration and feelings of deprivation simmer, only to scream out now. Sibling rivalry leads to envy and greed toward each other,[7] whereas generosity is related to gratitude. Adult children who have experienced good-enough parenting have feelings of inner wealth and they share with others.

Envy recedes into the background if we can identify with another person's happiness. When we have dealt with our feelings of anger and aggression, we are more willing to identify with others and share in their experiences. That means dealing with unwanted feelings of competition, rivalry, greed, and envy of siblings. Camille's story illustrates these feelings.

Camille the Caregiver

When I first met Camille, her unblemished complexion was naturally radiant, or so it seemed. Sun-streaked locks adorned her unlined oval face. She wore a pale green casual, yet chic, outfit that matched her eyes. Nothing looked studied, but it was.

Camille was obsessed with appearances, how she looked, and what she said to others. She explained that she wanted people to like her. She took great pains to look just so, and to be polite and sweet to everyone. What she said about her sister Janine wasn't exactly polite or sweet. Camille felt relief when her sister moved to Paris. Now that their mother was gravely ill, Janine returned home on a visit.

"I'll bet you must be thinking I look old, with my dark circles and wrinkles." Camille's superficial self-scrutiny was at work. Her composure was faltering and she seemed harried. She was beginning to look her age and she did not like it.

"I didn't have time to put on makeup and I'm a mess." She was distraught.

"What's going on?" I inquired.

"It's chaos again. Janine's back on a visit and we're fighting again. She aggravates the life out of my mother and me. I really think she gave my mother her first heart attack. And now she wants to finish her off." Camille blamed her sister.

"What are they fighting about now?" I asked.

"They're not. My mother's too weak to fight with her. If it were up to Janine, she'd still be at it." Camille tried to stay calm.

"That must be rough for you as the sole caregiver," I joined her.

"I'm stressed out and can't take Janine. She wants to help. Who needs her? She's nothing but trouble. Her life's a piece of cake compared to mine. I have all the burden and responsibility," Camille complained."

"It sounds like you resent her. Yet, you won't accept help from her," I confronted her.

"In a way I do resent her. But, she'd only worsen things if she got more involved. I wished she'd go back to Paris. I love my mother and although it's a strain, I want to do it myself." She was candid.

"Along with the stress are you finding satisfaction in caring for your mother?" I inquired.

"Yeah, while my mother's a burden, I take pleasure in taking care of her." She smiled.

"That's good. I wonder what sort of childhood you had?" I searched for history to make connections to the present.

"It was perfect, my mother and I were close. Janine was always jealous of our relationship. She claimed I was my mother's favorite. I don't know about that. I think my brother was her favorite. Janine was a wild teenager; she smoked, drank, and dated bad-boy types. My mother was furious with her and they fought a lot." Camille's face contorted in rage as she attacked her sister mercilessly.

"How about you?" I wanted her to focus on her self.

"I was different. I dressed appropriately and dated nice guys. My mother liked the boys, and also the man I married." Camille seemed pleased with her self.

"So, you behaved in ways that your mother approved of and your sister rebelled. And you're still trying to please others, whereas your sister could care less. You and Janine both have a close, but very different relationship with your mother. Your bond with your mother is affectionate, whereas Janine's bond is fraught with discord," I interpreted.

"I have a good life, nice friends, and a home. Janine made a mess of her life and she wants to mess up mine. She's divorced, working full time, and her son's an alcoholic." Camille did not understand her sister's plight one bit. The old rivalry got in the way.

"So, you fared better than her in many ways," I commented.

"In some ways yes, in other ways no. She doesn't suffer from depression and anxiety like I do." Camille showed insight.

"Do you think envy's in the picture?" I probed.

"Yeah, she envies my lifestyle. Actually I had a great life up until Mom got sick. I would've managed but Janine makes life hell. I know that caring for my mother is the right thing to do. It makes me feel good about my self." Camille got back on track.

"So helping her is helping you. I notice you pride yourself on being a moral person," I remarked.

"Yes, I think I'm moral. My sister's just the opposite. She's an embarrassment, the way she dresses. She's so rude. She claims she's just being honest. Hah!" Camille bashed her sister.

"So, you're decidedly more polite. While Janine's life is hard, she doesn't answer to anyone. Unlike you, she's not trapped by self-conscious scrutiny in order to garner approval. She's a free spirit. Are you ever envious of her?" I confronted her again.

"Envious of her, you must be kidding." She was enraged with me now. I hit a sensitive spot.

A lot of unfinished family business that quietly lay dormant became vociferous. Camille and Janine assumed the good girl/bad girl dichotomy early on in life. Each sister competed for mother's attention in her own way. Camille's obsession about appearances and Janine's disregard for social niceties were equally debilitating.

The emotional tie between Camille and her mother was far more satisfying, so she volunteered to care for her. And she refused her sister's help. The satisfaction she got in assuming the burden dovetailed with her need to live up to her ideal self as a caring, moral person. Despite the satisfaction she derived from her role as caregiver, Camille resented her sister. Envy and competition resurfaced.

Further in therapy we uncovered Camille's mother's dark side. Much like Camille, her mother was self-centered and focused on other people's opinion of her. When Camille came to this realization, she countered her idealization of her mother. She became aware of her deprivation, greed, and envy of her sister. Each sibling was deprived of a true sense of self; Janine fled from her self, whereas Camille found a false self in the approval of others.

Owning her loathsome qualities helped Camille feel more integrated and courageous. Her saccharine demeanor found richer expression in assertive behavior and, when necessary, confrontational behavior. She lost some friends, but gained far more as a real woman. Unlike her former shallow relationships, her new ones took on a more meaningful, authentic quality, and her depression and anxiety were ameliorated. Also, the compassion she gained for her sister's and her own shortcomings augured well for their relationship.

DIFFERENCES THAT DIVIDE

Differences in style, personality, and decision making can be enriching or divisive. Family history and prior relationship with parents hold center stage. Perceptions of relationships with parents are related to provision of care. Thus, siblings with divergent views of their relationships have feelings about providing care that are poles apart. Families with good parenting skills spawn children who are more likely to cooperate. Early deprivation, abuse, or neglect leads to envy and greed in siblings. Instead of sharing and cooperating with siblings, criticism or intolerance of each other's views prevails.

Coping styles may vary. So while one sibling obsesses over the illness of parents, another withdraws or avoids. Some adult children are overly protective and paternalistic and take over.[8] Others have a laissez-faire attitude, take a back seat, and leave the driving to their siblings. Position and role in the family play into the equation. Youngest children perceive their role differently from oldest or middle children. The beloved child manages differently from the child who felt like a scapegoat. While rewriting history is not possible, new history could be in the making. Differing views and attitudes are respected when heard with an empathic ear. Some of these dynamics are illustrated in the following scenario.

Brother's Keeper

Richard was the older of two brothers. Growing up, Richard's mother was plagued with bouts of debilitating depression, coupled with psychotic thinking. His father was a workaholic and rarely home. As far back as he could remember, Richard took on the role of the responsible, protective older brother to Paul. Although they worked together, Richard ran their real estate business. He described Paul as a playboy, who charmed the female customers. Paul brought business into the firm and Richard did the administrative work. Richard handled complaints, did the deals and the paperwork. His personality was diametrically opposite to Paul's. Whereas Richard was anal and detail oriented, Paul was carefree and loose as a goose.

Their differences worked for them in business; each recognized the other's strengths and shortcomings. They set up a division of labor that complemented each other. All was well until their father became impaired by a stroke. He lost his speech and movement on his right side. Richard took charge of his father's care and ordered the nurses around; his brother stayed out of the way.

"I'm so furious with Paul. He's always gotten away with murder." Richard was enraged.

"I thought you told me he carried his weight in the business, that you had settled into different, but complementary roles," I reminded him.

"If I said so, I don't feel like that now. I've always looked out for little Pauly. He won't help me with Dad. His excuse is he never learned how to take care of anyone. He says that I have. He's right. I took care of Paul all my life. It's over." His frustration got the better of him.

"Do you think he's unfit for the job?" I inquired about his expectations.

"Yeah, he's unfit for this job all right. The hell with him, I can do it myself!" He exploded.

"Maybe your negative prophecy is fulfilled. You predict he won't be up for the job and you show it. He picks up your negative prediction and acts to confirm it," I interpreted.

We worked on Richard's negative fortune-telling style, with ways to change his views and expectations of his brother. Richard became aware that taking charge of Paul gave him a false sense of power, and even now, when he complained bitterly about the inequity in the relationship, Richard still felt superior. Richard cast himself as the responsible, competent adult and Paul as the feckless child from whom he could never expect help.

Changing his perceptions was paramount for Richard to have a more equal, cooperative relationship with his brother. Finding other areas in which Richard would excel and feel powerful was in the offing. Richard's playful side was disavowed, while Paul enacted it. Addressing this in therapy, with the aid of dreams, we were pleasantly surprised to find that Richard's fantasies about the soft life included a bikini-clad gal serving him margaritas on the beach, while another lovely massaged his body. Others caring for him served to make Richard feel powerful. He discovered that fun was not the exclusive territory of his brother; indeed, he unconsciously harbored theses same wishes. Upon embracing these needs, he was able to see his brother in a better light. And his attitude changed. No longer did he bark at Paul when he did not help; instead he revealed his soft, vulnerable side. Richard let Paul know how overwhelmed and tired he felt, and Paul responded by taking over.

POWER PLAYS

Trying to get others to do it your way is a power play. Contrary to outward appearance of strength, rigid commands indicate underlying weakness. Flexibility and power sharing show strength. Not only are relationships enhanced, elderly or ill parents are better served. Life for frail people is hard enough; fighting among their adult children makes it harder.

Assuming too much responsibility brings resentment from others. Indeed, in the preceding case, Paul felt incompetent and resented his brother who assumed all the power. Richard was playing the martyr and Paul felt powerless and small. Condemning his brother to "hell," Richard anointed himself with sainthood. Richard's attitude antagonized Paul and further obstructed cooperation.

RESPECTING BOUNDARIES

Each family has its own thumbprint. Some families are enmeshed, with unclear, fuzzy boundaries that are constantly broken. Other families have strict, rigid boundaries, which keep family members distant from each other. Either type is problematic when caring for aging parents. Optimal boundaries are permeable, so that family members respect each other's privacy, but call on each other at times of need. In the Richard and Paul case, permeable boundaries at work facilitated progress. Not so at home. Placing a rigid boundary around his father and himself, Richard excluded Paul.

Enmeshed families are overly emotional and lack self-containment. Siblings who are too close lose their privacy and feel suffocated. The contrast is the feelings of alienation when family members are distant from each other. In a close-knit family with permeable boundaries, siblings have learned to care for each other and to respect each other's privacy. They go in and out of boundaries and reach out to siblings for help without feeling they are violating boundaries. They celebrate joyous occasions together and are there for each other in suffering.

The Burden Is on You

Out of life's school of war:
What does not destroy me,
makes me stronger.

Friedrich Nietzsche

The going gets rough when you are the only one available to care for your aging, infirm parent. No one else volunteers; they live in other parts of the country, they are too busy, too embroiled in their own lives, or just not interested. So, you are the chosen. One of my overwrought patients, Gilda, pleaded with God.

The Golden Girl

"God, I know I'm a Jew and we're the chosen people. Maybe this once, you could choose someone else." Gilda laughed through her tears.

"I can imagine how you feel," I commiserated with her.

"I shouldn't complain. I've always been Dad's favorite and stayed close to home. I led a charmed life. He loved me and called me his golden girl." Gilda stroked her golden blonde hair, which cascaded over her shoulders and onto her flowered summer frock. I could picture her picking flowers in a Monet garden. Suddenly I realized I had strayed from her depiction of an idyllic life. Was it envy?

"Your life was idyllic. Most people would envy you, but I can see where it's a problem. Because of it, you feel you're not entitled to complain now; instead, you should suffer in silence," I reflected.

"There's no one to help with decisions, research, or to share time. My brother lives in Texas and my sister's in Israel. So it falls on me. To top it off, my father's changed. He's stubborn, abusive, and childish. I have to repeat myself over and over, and he complains that I'm not listening to him. He just accused me of stealing his money. I want to be patient, but how much can I take?" She recounted her tale of woe.

"So you feel alone and overwhelmed," I observed.

"I am alone. I lost my husband two years ago, my children are doing their thing and so are my sister and brother." She wept.

"You could use nursing help for your father. Have you considered that option?" I suggested.

"It's not an option. Dad won't let anyone near him, only me. I told you I was the chosen." She laughed again.

"Guess what. You're not Superman or Superwoman. Even Superman had Lois Lane and the Lone Ranger had Tonto." I joined in the game.

"They were willing and able. My case is different." Gilda stubbornly held onto her martyrdom.

"Yeah, you've doomed yourself to suffer. Does it get you a better place in Heaven?" I asked, and she chuckled.

We worked on Gilda's guilty feelings, coupled with her fears of loneliness that interfered with reaching out for help. Her attachment to her father was intense in its own right, growing fiercer when her husband died and the children, now grown, moved on with their lives. Her father was all she had left; when he was gone, she would be alone. Not only that, she was next in line. So she hung on for dear life, denying her loneliness and death.

Tackling the existential issues of facing death was a harsh departure from her idyllic childhood. Nevertheless, her early loving childhood gave her a firm foundation of trust in others. Gilda was not going to give up on living and die with her father; instead she chose to live. One day she announced that like it or not, she hired a nursing aide and was taking the night off to go to a bridge group and dinner with friends. Her guilty feelings arose, but her wish to live fully and richly helped to allay them.

Aside from availability, there are other reasons that people volunteer. Love is one reason. Although Gilda volunteered out of necessity, another factor weighed in heavily. She had experienced a long-term close, loving tie with her father.

Attachment begins early in childhood and continues throughout a lifetime, even if separated by passage of time or distance.[1] There is more to it than that. Recent research indicates that close attachment throughout life is not dependent on whether you have been deprived or nurtured, but how you perceive the past—how you construct it in your memory.[2] So, if you perceive that your parents were always there for you, you feel love, obligation, or duty. The reverse holds true. The glasses you wear are rose-colored, dark, or distorted. Exchanging them for clear glasses is easier said than done.

Chances are that you are less likely to participate fully if you perceive a history of conflict between parent and you.[1] Yet, there has been evidence that you may volunteer despite a history of conflict.[3] A perceived love-hate relationship spurs you on to resist at first and then to go for it. Despite memories of harsh, cruel insults, when parents are frail, you may see them in a different light. They do not seem so threatening and the sting of their words does not smart as before.

RESENTMENT

Resentment toward family members who do not volunteer gets in the way of asking for help. Your siblings have never really been close to your parents and you are assuming they are not interested now. So you do not reach out and you do not get help. That is what is known as a self-fulfilling prophecy; such was the case with Richard. He assumed his brother could not and would not help, so unwittingly, he pushed him away.

If you perceive that you have always had a close, loving relationship with parents, you may assume greater responsibility than warranted. The burden leaves you feeling exhausted. A most unwanted feeling that arises when your parent finally dies may come as a surprise; you may feel elated, rather than grief-stricken.[4] Irene's case deals with burdensome feelings.

Irate Irene

Irene resented her brother for dodging his responsibilities. To top it off, Irene perceived her mother as never responding to her emotional needs. She remembered her mother as critical and demeaning, and Irene felt like the black sheep of the family. As for her brother, he was the apple of her mother's eye. Irene was a slight, shy woman, fearful of taking risks, whereas her brother thrived on challenges.

Irene lived alone and her self-esteem was in the toilet. She was lonely, depressed, and angry. Caring for an elderly, demanding mother, who never cared for her, taxed her to the limit.

"I didn't know what to expect. She's become so unreasonable; she wants me to give up my life for her. It's not like she ever did that for me. My mother's a Russian countess, in her own head that is. She was always self-absorbed; the world turned around her and her favorite child, my brother. She doted on him and he never assumed responsibility for anything. She did everything for him, so he didn't have to lift a finger. They were so tight. So, where is he now?" she uttered.

"So, you resent your brother," I noted.

"I'm furious with him." Irene was indeed enraged.

"Have you tried to enlist his help?" I suggested.

"He wouldn't help. Anyhow, I live closer to her," she retorted angrily.

"So what?" What do you think about delegating some responsibility to him?" I suggested.

"You're right. He could help. He lives in a suburb, not in Siberia." Her anger had abated somewhat.

In the following sessions, pride shone in Irene's face. She took a risk. Irene assigned duties to her brother, which he agreed to fulfill. She asserted herself, got a positive response, and felt better about herself.

GOING IT ALONE OR GETTING HELP

You are approaching burnout. Relief would be welcome. Your parent, however, refuses to go to a nursing home or even accept nursing help. Or funds may not be available for extra help. You are feeling the strain. You are on edge, crying a lot or having trouble sleeping. Although you are the sole caretaker, you need not be alone in the process. Going it alone is a lonely road. It behooves you to dig down into the far reaches of your psyche to plumb your motivations for undertaking this lonely path. Some people believe that no one else can do the job, and try to prove their point. You may want to reconsider this position. Surprisingly, when you ask in an inviting way, people are willing to help. Mabel's case illustrates these issues.

Able Mabel

The patient prior to Mabel heard my two kitties clamoring to come into the therapy room. He requested their appearance, so I let them in. After the session, I scooped them up and placed them out of the room. Alas, longhaired Persians tend to leave hair behind them. Mabel spotted the stray hairs and quickly brushed them off the sofa. She did a good job.

"Mabel, are you for hire?" I realized that I experienced her act as condescending.

"It's just that I can't stand messiness," she explained.

Mabel was the super housekeeper, super mom, and super fencing coach. Despite the children's sloppiness, the house was spic and span. She was also the consummate hostess, doing all the cooking, serving, and cleaning up by herself. Although her three sisters offered help, she declined, telling them she had everything under control. She complained that her sisters did not do things the way she liked, and that she would rather do it herself. Needless to say, Mabel had no time for herself. She felt anxious and exhausted even before her father's debilitating stroke. Yet, she volunteered to care for him, and once again Mabel refused help from anyone.

"You'd think they'd appreciate that Dad is living with me and I'm taking care of him, but no. Alice takes things for granted, Cornelia's snotty, and Roslyn was outright rude to me on Sunday at the barbecue. As usual, I got no help from anyone." Mabel protested her family's lack of cooperation.

"Rather than feel grateful, your sisters feel resentment toward you," I interpreted, recalling my feelings of her cleaning up after my kitties.

"Why?" Mabel was in the dark.

"I know you mean well, but perhaps your sisters see you as taking over and leaving them out of things," I interpreted.

"I don't like the way they do things. If you saw Alice's house you'd know what I mean. She lives in a pigsty. Cornelia's head is somewhere else, and Roslyn lives out of town." Mabel found excuses for her refusal of help.

"They may have feelings about your position of power." I felt her sisters' anger toward her.

"Power, what power?" Mabel was angry with me. I could see why, as I delivered a powerful punch.

"I can see why you're angry with me. I felt compelled to protect your sisters." I explained my role in the enactment.

"Well, you don't have to. They're tough; they get nasty and explode plenty." Mabel's rage turned to her sisters.

Able Mabel was not able to maintain a give-and-take with her sisters. She decided to go it alone and prove her competence. Eventually, she felt so exhausted by the burden that she accepted help. Her sisters may not have done things exactly like she did, but she agreed that they did things well enough. With less bickering and more loving interactions among his children, her father improved his mood.

Of course, not everyone has a relative living nearby, who would help when called upon, as in Irene and Mabel's cases. There are a number of ways to communicate with others, including email and long distance calls, both of which have special rates. Research and decision making may be shared long distance, even if providing care is not.

The internal struggle about alternative living arrangements is eased when you are not the only one to make decisions. When others participate in making serious decisions, there is a greater feeling of comfort.

Long-Distance Caring

The difficult we do immediately.
The impossible takes a little longer.
David Ben-Gurion

The flip side of living too close to your elderly parents is living too far from them. Relatives taking the brunt of the responsibility resent you, as in the preceding cases. You may be torn by responsibilities in your life and feelings about your parents. Moving closer is not a viable or prudent solution.

YOUR EMOTIONAL CONFLICT

Even though other demands are pressing, when you are not at your parent's side, feelings of shame and guilt plague you. You are torn between loyalties to your parents and troubled children, an ill spouse, or a job. The prior relationship with parents may have been problematic, so you are unwilling to come to the side of an ill parent. You may fear that a resumption of the former conflict is inevitable and would only worsen matters. Such is the following case.

Carol in Conflict

Carol loved her mother, but always clashed with her. Carol was now rent between her feelings of caring for her ailing mother or keeping watch on her wild adolescent daughter. Not only that, Carol was divorced and struggled to survive financially, so she could not leave her job.

"I'm so tired, yet I can't sleep. I worry about my mother and my poor sister who's assumed the burden. I also worry about Chelsea, who's smoking pot, dressing like a hooker, and cutting classes," Carol explained.

"So, you're racked with worry and rent in half," I commented.

"Yeah, when I think about my mother and sister in California and me in New York, I feel guilty. I should be there with them. Then I consider my daughter's needs and my job, and I have this pull to stay here. I also feel sorry for my sister. She's doing the right thing and I'm not." Carol did not like herself.

"So you feel conflicted, ashamed, and guilty. What do you think your sister feels?" I inquired.

"I think she's doing great. She's never been the strong one, but she sure has rallied to my mother's side. She's amazing. I admire her a lot." Carol gave me a lukewarm smile.

"Maybe she's not so poor after all, maybe she derives some satisfactions from her role as hands-on caregiver," I noted.

"I guess she does. She was always big on duty and doing the right thing," Carol conceded.

"So she's getting a chance to do that," I continued.

"It's still hard for her." Carol empathized with her sister.

Carol's view of herself as a good person was damaged, whereas her sister's was intact. Sleepless nights and worry-filled days sapped her energies and she felt tired, depressed, and anxious. She also felt powerless. Her sister had the bulk of the burden, yet she derived something positive out of the role. When Carol arrived at this realization, she did not feel so torn by her loyalties.

Indeed caring for elderly parents is difficult, but it is also satisfying. Many people carry an image of themselves as good people, who do the right thing, as was the case for Carol's sister. Caregivers are able to gratify their goals of doing the right thing. The caregiver role may fulfill their ideals and standards of themselves as good, giving, and caring people.[1,2]

Aware of her sister's benefits, Carol felt some relief from her guilty feelings that sapped her energies and paralyzed her. Feeling freer, Carol searched possible ways that she could be more involved with her mother's care, without sacrificing her child's needs or the family's financial needs. She called her sister more often, researched the Internet, emailed her information, and flew in for some important decision-making appointments with doctors.

POWER LOST AND FOUND

When someone else is assuming responsibility for your parent's care, you may feel powerless. Indeed, you have little control over your parents' health. In the preceding case, Carol felt a loss of power with both her strong-willed daughter and her frail elderly mother. If she left her job, she would be penniless, so she would lose out even more.

Carol and I discussed ways to participate long distance and to feel more empowered. By implementing some of our ideas, she felt better about her roles as a mother, daughter, and sister.

Consider scheduling trips for important decisions so you may be in on the process. While that is not always possible, other forms of close contact may be viable. Keeping in close communication with siblings is a way to be part of the process. You can do research on treatments and consult with knowledgeable professionals and doctors. Then you may share your findings with your caretaker sibling. I have found that email is efficient, whereas the telephone may feel more immediate. Check it out.

Handle with Care

We make a living by what we get,
we make a life by what we give.

Winston Churchill

I want to share some therapy tools of my armamentarium to help you take control of your inner states so that you can better provide care with kindness. As a psychoanalyst, I use relational psychoanalytic thought as my launch pad, from whence my creativity springs. In working with young children and with some elderly people, I have been stretched to new frontiers of imagination.

There are vast differences between these two groups; whereas children are in the process of becoming who they will be, elderly people are in the process of remembering who they were. So they are at opposite ends of the lifespan. Nevertheless, they react to momentary joys and discomforts in some similar ways. Elderly, ill parents have a tendency to regress to childish behavior, which may be discomfiting, to say the least. The role reversal leaves you feeling at wits' end. I will toss out some ideas to help you understand their plight and to inspire your imagination. Use your creative powers to expand, enhance, or change them at will.

COMPASSION

A man, to be greatly good, must imagine intensely
and comprehensively; he must put himself in the
place of another and many others; the pains and
pleasures of his species must be his own.

Percy Bysshe Shelley

Without feeling compassion, therapeutic techniques are mechanical and ring a false note. Compassion is the underpinning of authentic therapeutic care. In part, compassion implies a deep feeling of sympathy for your elderly parents. When you put yourself in their place and share their feelings of suffering, you are in a better place to help and be more supportive. Understanding where they are coming from helps you to gain more patience. Hence, your guilt and stress are ameliorated. A more benign perception of your parents and your self stabilizes you.

As discussed earlier, the self is a relational construct. Your previous relationship with your parent is reversed. The new relationship has transformed your old self and that of your parent. When parents order you around and try to consume every waking moment, how can you feel compassion? You just want to scream or run away—not exactly welcome wishes that lead to sympathy. Instead you end up feeling inept and worthless. Rather than compassion for them, you feel self-pity.

Take a moment out and I will try to clarify some of your parents' plight. Your infirm parents are communicating something to you. Remember my discussion of quantum physics? I wrote about changes in one subatomic particle that occurred simultaneously in another particle in another laboratory. The principle is akin to unconscious communications that travel from one person to another and produce concurrent changes. The feelings you experience inside of you are those of your parents. You experience their feelings of ineptitude and worthlessness.

Many adult children caring for elderly parents whom I see in therapy protest angrily about their parents. Let us consider the concept of unconscious communications again. Some elderly people are confused. Your parents may fear they are losing their minds. In turn, you feel you are losing your mind, that your aging parents are driving you crazy. Maybe they are. Indeed, they are communicating their feelings of going crazy to you.

How often do you blame your self for not having been a better child, more grateful, and of not doing enough now? How about feeling shame and guilt? Whose thoughts and feelings are they anyway? Are they yours or your parents?

Some ill, older people blame themselves for their illness, that they did not take good care of themselves. They may not have heeded early symptoms of disease. Or they may have practiced an unhealthy lifestyle. In retrospect, smoking, eating high-fat foods, or drinking may have yielded momentary pleasures. When older people recognize the havoc they wrought on themselves, they may blame themselves. They feel ashamed of their prior excesses, no matter how seductive they were in their youth. Also, in old age, ill parents often feel they are a burden to their children. Being a burden may bring guilt.[1]

Some older people facing death may feel guilty about how they treated loved ones. Reviewing their lives, parents may feel ashamed about certain selfish behavior toward their children. They have pursued their own interests to the detriment of healthy development of their children. Other parents may have been disparaging and harsh. Although they were trying to improve their children, now, close to death, parents shrink from their critical behavior. They may blame themselves for their children's poor sense of self-worth, so they project their own feelings of shame, guilt, and worthlessness on to their children.

Another basis for feelings of shame and rage is how people deal with their aging process. No matter the stooped shoulders, the sagging skin, or failing health, many elderly people insist on seeing themselves as twenty-six, still young, vigorous, and healthy.[2] When aged, ill parents see their children's youth, they remember their own youthful bodies, and feel shame about their frail, deteriorated body. Narcissistic rage is a method employed to ward off disgrace.[3] Elderly parents use all sorts of remedies to deny their aging, insults to their self-esteem, assaults on their bodies and minds, and demands on them to cooperate. Hence, they withdraw, sulk, or fling vitriolic attacks on their children. These are unconscious communications that are painful and hard to bear as seen in the following group interactions.

Moving Targets

"My father's driving me crazy!" Neil uttered in consternation. In the next breath, "I have no patience for him. He's crazy."

"I feel like you do. I should feel sorry for her, but I don't. She's always been crazy, now she's over the top. She's blaming me for everything that went wrong in my life. 'Why'd you marry Allen?' she asks me. 'The minute I laid eyes on him, I saw he was no good,' she's reminding me for the hundredth time. 'What kind of parent are you anyway? How come Roberta's not married yet? How come you can't find a job?' Those are a few of her gems. I want to kill her," Jill shouted in frustration. Her mother was projecting her feelings of blame regarding her own deficits onto Jill. So the target of blame moved from mother to daughter.

"My father's hateful and sticks it to me. He likes to read about history, so I bought him the latest book on presidents. Without so much as glancing at the book, he said he didn't like it. I asked why and he said, 'because you never knew what I liked, you're not interested in me, only yourself, you're selfish.' Actually, he's never shown any interest in me; he only thinks of himself. " Marvin was steaming. This was clearly a projection of feelings.

"I have mixed feelings about my mother. I love her, but I blame her for her cancer. My mother smoked her whole life. Even after being diagnosed with lung cancer, she continued to smoke. Now, it's too late. The cancer's metastasized to her liver and she's got a few weeks left. I feel guilty about my angry feelings towards her." Carl was crying openly. Carl's mother also felt guilty about smoking and she cried a lot. Carl swallowed these guilty feelings.

"I also have a love/hate relationship with my mother. You should see how she treated my father. She was a ball buster and he kowtowed to her. She demeaned him and said I was lazy like him, that he never amounted to anything and that I was just like him. Like she amounted to something! Actually Dad made a good living and she never worked. He was an insurance broker. I guess I followed in his footsteps; I'm a financial planner. But we weren't good enough for her. We used to have vicious fights. Now she has heart disease; she's frail and withdrawn. It's a terrible thing to say, but I miss the fights. If only I could go back and erase some of the nasty things I said to her." Michele lowered her head.

Michele felt despondent and guilty. Her mother felt the same way. Was this an unconscious communication from mother to daughter? Perhaps her mother's depression was related to her guilt about her domineering and disparaging behavior to her family.

"My dad's always been a dapper guy, everything matched. He even had a face-lift fifteen years ago, which was unusual for men back then. He finally looks elderly, but he won't accept it. He's fuming about his arthritis, that he's lost his hair and is wearing glasses. His health is good. His balance is off and when he walks, he falls. The last spill was nasty, so I took him to the orthopedist. He did an MRI and said that everything was normal for his age. The doctor recommended a three-pronged cane. Dad threw the cane at me and swore at the doctor. 'How could you suggest I use this bloody contraption; it's for old people.' And then he spat at me." Earle was exacerbated. Rage moved from his father to him.

"My mother won't accept her aging either, only she clings to me. She keeps calling me every minute to 'do this, do that.' I can't get away from her for even one minute. I'm running from pillar to post and I feel powerless," Maria sobbed. Her mother felt powerless to slow the aging process.

"There's a strong tie between you and your parents, and blame gets shifted from them to you. You're the target of their projections. The burden may weigh you down. Maybe it's time to divest your selves of excess baggage," I addressed the group.

How do you handle the projected rage, the hateful assaults? Instead of fighting them, join them. In psychoanalytic parlance we call it "going with the resistance." Mirroring or merging with parents may disarm them. Elderly people feel alone and fear dying alone. A feeling of being understood and unity with you goes a long way. To mirror or merge with another, you must resonate with their inner worlds. Rather than getting defensive or striking back, try strolling in their slippers. Listen to your imagination and form loving links with them. You could try to join them and exclaim outrage at the unfairness of life. Your parents will probably stop and listen. Or you might cry along with them and impart your sadness to them. You both may feel better after a good cry.

Let's go back to Jill's dilemma. I posed a question that reflected the idea of mirroring and merging.

"Jill, do you think your mother feels like a loser and is projecting that onto you?" I inquired.

"I hadn't thought of it that way. Maybe," Jill nodded in assent.

"What would happen if you agreed with your mother and told her she's right, that you are a loser?" I was asking her to merge with her mother.

"She'd tell me how great I am. 'Look what you made of yourself, you're a great mother and your kids love you.' That's what she'd say," Jill laughed.

"So, if you went along with her, you'd disarm her. And she'd feel comforted," I clarified.

Marvin's relationship with his father was laden with conflict.

"How do you think you could disarm your father?" I asked Marvin.

"Instead of telling him he's selfish and doesn't even know me. I could say that maybe he's interested in history, but not this book. I could also agree with him, that I'm not always such a thoughtful person. He'd probably disagree and say that I was terrific. Go figure." Marvin picked up on my suggestion to Jill.

"Carl and Michele, you guys have something in common—your feelings of dejection and guilt. And your parents seem to have the same feelings, so you've merged with them. Maybe it would be helpful to be the mirror for their feelings. Also, let them know that we can't erase the past; what's done is done," I addressed them.

"Earl, you could try empathizing with your father's rage at his aging process," I suggested.

"Give me some hints, I need help," Earle asked of me.

"I think your father's rage stems from his shame about his aging. What do you think would happen if you declared emphatically that 'Life isn't fair. It's a shame you have to grow older.' It beats the alternative," I smiled.

"He'd probably cry and I'd cry with him. I hate to think of losing him." Earle was in tears.

"So, you'd match his outrage with humor and merge with him in despair," I interpreted.

"Maria, I think your mother fears dying alone, so she clings and demands constant attention." I clarified her mother's fears. "Merge with her fear and offer her some comfort. You've indicated that she's religious, so you could tell her you'll see her on the other side.[2] Then she won't be so scared," I offered.

"My mom is religious, so she might like it. I hope it works." Maria seemed brighter.

Once the group members had a better understanding of their parents' plight, and that their parents' feelings of helplessness, depression, and rage were being projected onto them, they could feel more compassionate. Instead of fighting their parents, they joined them. By doing so, they brought levity to a sad situation, and felt more empowered and hopeful.

LIFE REVIEW

Elderly, ill parents often withdraw into themselves in depression or strike out in rage. They are no longer living; instead, they exist in misery or tremble with fear. Life review is a process in which both of you engage in a mutually pleasurable activity. The interaction gives parents a sense of being alive and resuming the parental role. As parents, they are informing you; as the child, you are learning from them. Sharing memories is a wonderful avenue for merger without feeling suffocated.

Uppermost is the idea of therapeutic care, so it is important for you to guide the process toward fond memories. Encourage your parents to remember their positive attributes. Your parents, albeit not perfect, may have been attentive parents, good educators, moral teachers, or role models of healthy values and ambitions. As an adult child, you have the advantage over other caregivers. Chances are, you know more about your parents than anyone else; you may be surprised to find areas not formerly revealed.

Some elderly parents are all too willing to recount colorful tales of yesteryear. I have found that people suffering from dementia and early stages of Alzheimer have some intact long-term memory. Shame about loss of short- term memory is mediated by pride in long-term memory. I have seen cases where elderly people get carried away, embellish, and even tell tall tales. But so what? Lending an ear to their fantasies is fun. Be prepared. Since short-term memory is impaired, they forget what they have told you and repeat the same or altered versions of the stories. Again, so what? It beats withdrawal or rage.

Other elderly parents need prodding. I would suggest you find old photos and use them as a stimulus for memory retrieval and sharing. If you are familiar with a parent's favorite music, it may kindle good memories. If not, ask your parent what his or her favorite music was when growing up. Retrieving this music may be fun. Sharing in family gossip sometimes works, especially if it harks back to younger years. Nellie is such a case.

Head Nurse Nellie

Maria and Ed were perplexed with how to help their elderly mother Nellie. Although she was in a good nursing home, Nellie refused to interact with other residents. She was in good physical health, but suffered from depression and dementia. Maria and Ed decided to seek my help. The only information I got about Nellie was that in her youth she was a nurse.

"Nellie, I understand you were a nurse," I began.

"A head nurse." Nellie raised her head from its former drooping position.

"Where did you work?" I inquired.

"On a battleship. I worked with injured naval men. I was the head nurse." There was a twinkle in Nellie's eyes as she smiled. Maria commented that it was the first time she saw her mother smile in months.

"So, you knew just how to care for these wounded soldiers. After all, you were head nurse," I joined her.

"I had 130 men to care for. I was too busy to get married," she went on.

"Why marry one, when you can have 130 men?" I tried humor.

"I had 130 men on the ship at one time. They flirted and wanted me, but I was head nurse," she responded proudly.

"Did you flirt back, a little?" I asked.

"I didn't want to lead them on, or they'd get too excited. I'm not that kind of girl. Twenty guys proposed marriage, but I refused. I traveled a lot on the ships and saw different countries. I was in Japan, Germany, France, England, and Holland." Nellie was enjoying her prowess.

"Why tie yourself down to marriage, when you can be free to travel the world?" I mirrored her. You may call her stories fantasies, but they were her realities. She constructed her reality to suit her, and I united and merged with her.

"I had my pick of men. I was head nurse." She was pleased as punch with her self.

I reviewed the session with Maria and Ed, suggesting that they try engaging their mother, Nellie, in Life Review. Since they knew her far better than I did, they could draw on family memorabilia, old photos, music, and the like. They left feeling armed with some new tools for engagement with their mother. Sadly, Nellie passed away two months later; however, Maria and Ed reported that the quality of her life was enhanced and that they felt some satisfaction from their participation. With this knowledge, her death was somewhat easier to bear.

Harry and Hagar

My great uncle Harry lived to 104, was in excellent health, and shopped and cooked for himself. Come rain or shine, Harry was meticulously dressed with jacket, vest and tie. He resided alone in an apartment in Manhattan and walked thirty blocks daily. Like Nellie, Harry loved to review his former life and I loved to listen to his stories. Harry adored beautiful women and pursued them in his mind and in reality. At his deathbed, he was surrounded by a bevy of beautiful women.

Many of Uncle Harry's tales took on a sexual flavor. He often recounted biblical tales of aged Abraham, who slept with Sarah, his wife, and Hagar, a servant, many years his junior. Harry had his own Hagar. He befriended Lilly, an educated forty-five-year-old woman, who was visiting her psychologist in Harry's building. Harry was still writing letters to U.N members about social issues, and he enlisted her to do the typing. He treated her to fancy lunches and dinners, put her in a cab, and happily went home alone. Smiling, Harry told me that Lilly wanted to kiss him; but he refused, as he feared she would get too passionate and she could not satisfy him. His constructed reality was fantastic!

Uncle Harry was amazing. His verve was related to a blend of sexuality, constructed reality, wishes, intellect, and fond memories. He kept a letter from Eleanor Roosevelt in his inside jacket pocket. He loved to show it to me and retell the story of his active involvement with the U.N. He had a photo of Mrs. Roosevelt and himself on a park bench. After hearing his opinions on Social Security issues at a U.N. meeting, she invited him to join her on a park bench to continue their discussion. Recounting the story numerous times served to make Harry feel competent and important. He took pride knowing that a great lady had acknowledged him for participating in something meaningful.

CREATIVE CHILD THERAPY

Not all elderly infirm parents are as young in mind and cooperative as Nellie and Harry. Indeed, your parents may be childish or oppositional. Remember the parenting advice you got when your children were young? The goal was to help them behave in ways that were pleasant. A central theme was to facilitate the development of healthy self-esteem. Many elderly ill parents feel humiliated by their deterioration, and much of the childish behavior is related to that shame. I will toss out some ideas and you may improvise in order to apply them to your parents.

Positive Spin

Merging with the positive attributes and behaviors of elderly parents provides a sense of unity, comfort, and security. In addition, a focus on the positive enhances self-esteem. If your parents' behaviors are stubborn or reprehensible, do not rise to their level. Instead, ignore the behaviors, breathe deeply ten times, and wait until you both cool off. A former supervisor gave me some sound advice, which was to strike when the iron was cool. Then you are able to interact in a gentle and constructive manner. You may even employ humor. Indeed, humor that is not tinged with sarcasm is disarming.

When your parents' behaviors approach politeness, praise them. Let them know how heartwarming it is to see them behaving in social, cooperative ways. The applause you lavish on them facilitates their fragile self-esteem. And you may be surprised to see more favorable behavior. The idea is to reinforce the positive and ignore the negative. Whereas before they have gotten attention for childish behavior, now they get attention for more mature behavior. A caveat is in order here. Deprived of attention for negative behavior, elderly people's negative behavior may escalate. Hang in; it will subside.

LIMITS WITH LOVE

Setting limits implies permeable boundaries you place around you, so that you maintain a separate sense of self while caring for your parents. To set limits with love means knowing when to say "enough" and when to go into action.

When boundaries are fluid and meshed, you lose sight of limits and respond instantly to every complaint. Overdoing robs your parents of their sense of autonomy and they feel even more childish and enfeebled. In turn, you feel suffocated and exhausted. Rigid boundaries or limits set in stone are not the answer either. Too much distance leaves your parents feeling lonely and more fearful. And you feel guilty.

Limit setting is tricky. Knowing when to respond to complaints or when to ignore them comes with time. There is no one pat answer that fits all. Each relationship and personal story are unique. Trial-and-error learning entails awareness of what works and what does not. When an approach does not work, more of the same is not a good idea. Flexibility is the key.

PLAYING WITH PARANOIA

Ever try using logic with someone who holds firmly to illogical beliefs or paranoid delusions? It is next to impossible. To reiterate, if you cannot fight them, join them. Entering into their delusional system, you merge with them. Let your imagination run wild; draw on humor and play their game. Frolic in the playpen of fantasy and delusion. It may be great fun! The following scenario bears on these issues.

Perils of Paulette

"My mother Paulette has a heart condition, but that's not the problem. It's her head; she's gone crazy. Her mind was so sharp; she was a nutritionist and addressed audiences all over. Now she hardly eats, won't leave her bed, and talks crazy stuff to herself. She tells me the FBI is after her, that they think she's a terrorist, and that they're threatening to kill her. Her reason for abstaining from food is that she heard them say they're going to poison her. She fears perils all over." Lauren was distressed.

"How do you handle it?" I inquired.

"Poorly. I've tried everything; nothing works. I took her to a geriatric psychiatrist, who said that it's not uncommon for elderly people to have paranoid delusions. Dr. Stein prescribed an antipsychotic medication, but Mom's suspicious about him, and believes he's a party to the conspiracy against her. So, she refuses to take it." Lauren looked defeated.

"Lauren, you look lost," I reflected.

"I'm desperate. I try to talk some sense into her. I tell her there's no conspiracy against her, that it's all in her head. She yells back that there's nothing wrong with her head, that it's my head that's screwed up. I ask her for any evidence of the conspiracy and she tells me it's right in front of my nose. 'Don't you see it?' she screams. 'Are you trying to make me crazy?' she hollers. No matter how hard I try to set her thinking straight, she's convinced herself that I'm crazy and that she's not. Lately, I'm beginning to think she's right," Lauren smiled wryly.

"So, why not try going crazy with her?" I suggested.

"What do you mean?" she asked.

"What about letting go of your rational thinking and merging with her paranoid delusion?" I suggested.

"It sounds weird," Lauren responded.

"Uh huh, that's the idea; get weird like she does. Are you afraid you won't return to reality?" I inquired.

"No, I've been known to do some crazy things myself and to come back to reality. My choice of my last husband was a little crazy. I knew him for one month before I married him. He swept me off my feet. He was romantic and exciting and we did crazy, fun things together. I was drunk with love, but I had to sober up real fast. It wasn't even a month into the marriage when I learned he had another wife. He was a bigamist. I cried, screamed, and got an annulment." Lauren looked wistful.

"So, you were able to return to a more normal life. Do you long for some excitement?" I reflected her feeling state.

"I've got plenty, not the fun kind. I see what you're getting at. I could try telling her she's right, that she's so much more insightful than I am." Lauren was game.

"That's the spirit. You could amplify it by complimenting her sleuthing abilities, that she could spot Dr. Stein and that the telltale signs were all over. You could say, 'I'll bet his white gown is hiding dark, secret weapons, and that he prescribes poison,'" I continued.

"I could berate myself and say how stupid of me and how smart she was. I could emphasize that there's something wrong with my thinking. She'd probably dispute me and say that I was smart just like her. Who knows, maybe she'd even argue that Dr. Stein's a kind man and wouldn't do anyone harm." Lauren was having fun.

"You could suggest that she put her hypothesis to the test, by trying his medicine." I was also having fun.

"I could suggest we both hide under the covers so that we're safe. I could speak to an imaginary evil monster and beseech him not to attack us. My mother would probably tell me I was seeing things." Lauren was enjoying our play and left feeling excited. At the door, she came up with one more creative thought.

"I could tell her I won't eat the food either, that I was on a diet anyway. She thinks I'm too skinny, so she'd tell me the food's safe. I'd say it isn't and that she was right to avoid it. She'd probably break down and eat her meal to prove that it was safe for me to eat. Even if nothing works, I'll have fun with her." Lauren returned to reality.

Like Lauren, finding creative ways to play with paranoia by joining parents may disarm them. Most important, it will stretch your imagination and exercise your creative powers. Thrown into the responsible caretaker adult role, the inner child is squashed. Freeing your child spirit is life affirming. Try it; you may like it.

The Setting Sun

Emblems of mist and emblems of trees,
cast forever into the pools of night
                    Norman Finkelstein[1]

The dim, hushed light of twilight signals the onset of silent darkness.
The sun is setting on your parents. The final separation is replete with
loss and mourning. Although you have survived dark nights of the soul
in your lifetime, in this period of sorrow, you suffer anew. Suffering
brings greater dimension to our experience and helps us to be more
valiant and powerful. Nevertheless, the grieving process itself is not
about bravery or strength; it is about the sting of undiluted pain surging
through our veins.

THE FINAL SEPARATION

Intimate Attachment and Loss

Intimate attachments to other human beings are the hub around
which a person's life revolves, not only when he is an infant or
a toddler or a school child but throughout his adolescence
and his years of maturity as well, and on into old age.
                    John Bowlby[2]

The relationship between child and parent is an intimate attachment,
from early childhood to old age and afterward. The close relationship
with parents is singular; since it took years to build, it could take years
to let go.[3] Indeed, separation from intimate partners is a wrenching
innermost loss. Although repeated separation-individuation cycles
from parents are normal, they are, nevertheless, a lifelong struggle[4]

from womb to tomb.[5] Separations in service of growth and independence bring to mind bittersweet and often tender moments of joy tinged with sadness. Weaning from the breast, wobbly first steps taken away from mother, a teary departure for the first day of school, the first date, the first kiss, our wedding and the birth of our children, their weddings and the birth of our grandchildren: all separation-individuation steps, rehearsals for the final goodbye—death.

Every exhilarating step for independence is laden with poignant loss of the intimate parent-child attachment. But attachments do not stop at death—which can be somewhat comforting at this difficult time. Indeed, attachments continue through memories and internal processes.

One of these internal processes is called internalization, which means to take into our selves aspects of how parents related to us. Parental values, goals, attitudes, feelings, and behaviors make up the internal template for how we relate to our selves and others. Internalization occurs throughout the life cycle, especially when separated or when we lose parents.[6] Internalization is how we keep our parents inside our selves and how they continue to live on with us.

Children whose parents readily soothed their hurts find it easier to soothe their selves in time of crisis. People who have been fortunate enough to internalize parental calming may be able to draw on these images to comfort themselves. Still others, no matter the optimal childhood, will be inconsolable, missing the comforting maternal bosom and longing in vain for it. Alas, it is not to be, and they are left to endure this pain without them.

Adult children who lacked adequate soothing in childhood may have great difficulty in soothing themselves, and mourning is complicated by faulty internalized messages. They do not carry an internal representation of mother-child soothing, so this time may be fraught with fears of falling apart. Drawing on other sources is helpful. Taking a pit stop to reflect on one's strengths and ability to cope in prior crises helps one to feel more pulled together. Reaching out to empathic, soothing others brings comfort to inconsolable selves.

We internalize numerous messages from parents that live on after they have died. When parents have reinforced our achievements, we developed an ideal of our selves as high achievers and attempted to live up to that goal. The emphasis may have been on beauty and appearances, and an ideal self was built on a flimsy foundation. Or, it may have been on intelligence and competence, as in the following case.

Smart Sue and Beautiful Belle

A dark-eyed, auburn-haired beauty, Sue had a lot going for her. She had built a satisfying law practice and a side career as a nonfiction author. You would think she had developed a healthy self-image, but, sad to say, she had not.

"I've always been one of the smartest in the class; the kids nicknamed me Smart Sue. Unfortunately, I was the ugly duckling, so I wasn't popular," Sue explained some of her internal scripts.

"Well you've achieved a lot, so that being smart figures. Aside from innate intelligence, did you have early influences?" I was curious.

"My father was intellectual and praised my achievements. He emigrated from Poland as a teenager and didn't know a word of English. He survived a rough childhood, but he persisted. He was self-taught and read a lot of philosophy and politics. Dad had a moral imagination about the world." Sue was melancholy as she recalled her father's background.

"Well, you've taken that part of him inside of you. You've persevered and devoted your practice to freeing innocent people on death row. I'd call that a moral imagination." I mirrored her considerable gifts.

"He was a good man and my staunchest supporter. So losing him is like losing my eyesight. It's so sad. Nothing gives me pleasure now." Sue was despondent.

"So, you saw the world through his eyes, which death has closed. Indeed, it's sad, very sad. You're mourning the loss of someone you cherished." I reflected her feelings, as I felt sad inside.

"It's so hard. Now I have only Mom and Belle. My children are grown and on their own. My mother was always into superficiality and self-serving acts. It was how it looked to others, not what it meant. My mother adores Belle; she thinks they're more alike. Mom was a great beauty and still is; so is Belle. She was always popular, the boys chased her, and her nickname was Beautiful Belle. My mother told me that I resembled my dad, who she considered to be ugly. As an adult, I've tried to outgrow that ugly duckling image, but it still overshadows other aspects of my self. I've had plastic surgery to correct my nose and recently had a face-lift. I work out at the gym daily so my body is in shape. My head isn't, though." Sue was searching into her background for answers.

"You've been dealt a hand with some good cards and some bad cards. Maybe you need to do some reshuffling," I suggested. Sad Sue finally smiled.

"You're probably right. But, it's hard. Belle was born beautiful; she married a man who worships her and she enjoys a great social life. She was gorgeous naturally. I think she's smarter than me, but she was too anxious to take on challenges. I take them on repeatedly, so my life's a constant struggle," she explained.

"You persevere, succeed, and help the world. You've internalized a goal to achieve and that's how you'll keep your father inside of you now that he's dead. Good memories remain and are a source of comfort. Maybe it's time to delete the ugly message you've internalized from your mother," I interpreted.

"I'll try, but it's a part of me," she responded sadly.

We went on a journey to reshuffle the cards, so that the ace of diamonds would find its way to the top of the deck. Indeed, her father's legacy was a rich, meaningful existence and Sue had internalized his strengths. Her distorted view of her appearance, internalized from her mother, however, kept her from socializing and finding intimacy with others.

Her father's death brought home what she was missing in her life. Sue began to think about exploring the possibility of an intimate relationship with a new man. The two men in her life had not worked out, with both relationships ending in divorce. The first man cheated on her, which she attributed to her unappealing appearance, internalized from her childhood. The second man injured her self-esteem further by his self-centered ways and neglect of her feelings—a hurtful reminder of her mother.

Sue joined a therapy group of like-minded people struggling with self-esteem issues internalized from parents and later reinforced by devaluing partners. Countering faulty perceptions and looking into a clearer mirror, rational as it seems, met with emotional resistance. Feeling confused, Sue tested her negative self-perceptions with the group. She refrained from revealing her impressive profession to the group until later, so she would get feedback from them about her self, separate from her achievements. Would the group members love her simply for her self, her generosity, charm, and sensitivity to others? Or did she have to continue to impress with her accomplishments? Indeed Sue found that, unlike her judgmental mother, the group accepted, respected, and loved her solely for her self. Their values were closer to her father's.

This experience helped to summon her courage to explore other arenas, where she would continue to experience positive feedback. Hopes for finding love and intimacy were awakened. Keeping her father's affirming voice inside of her and discarding her mother's rejecting voice were goals that Sue continued to work on. Mourning was nevertheless sorrowful, but her new outlook helped Sue bear the grief.

Fusion Fantasies

Death reawakens the wish for merger—the oceanic feeling of oneness with parents of early childhood. In a renowned paper, "Mourning and Melancholia," Freud made the connection between melancholia and infantile love—the merger state with feelings of fusion between parent and child.[6] Freud described melancholia as a normal emotional reaction to the loss of a loved person. Symptoms of melancholia and mourning include depression, loss of interest in normal outside interests, and an intense devotion to the loved dead person.

Optimally, emotional reassurance and comfort were first derived from merger with a parent. The early merger state is the basis for intimacy, trust of others, and confidence that we get our needs gratified. Hence, loss of a parent implies not only sadness, but also a loss of the myth of absolute security, comfort, and power. This heart-wrenching passage is a central part of the mourning process. So, when separation-individuation stages have not been resolved, anxiety invades melancholy states as in Melanie's story.

Melancholy Melanie

When I first met Melanie, she was frisky and carefree. Wearing white socks, sneakers, and khaki shorts, she reminded me of a cheerleader. Melanie was working on her marriage, which was impacted by the overly close relationship with her mother. She did not make a move without consulting her mother. Her husband, Tom, complained that she was on the phone with her mother ten times a day, and she could not make a simple decision without her mother's approval. Melanie did not see it that way; she simply thought that they had a great relationship and that her husband was just jealous. So she shrugged off his criticisms and continued her merry way.

Now her mother was dying, Melanie was not exactly merry; she was depressed and anxious. She had seen the world as rosy, but she now saw everything as dismal and dark.

"My mother and I were so close; she was my best friend. I didn't make a decision without asking her. I'm totally unprepared for what's going on. I can't think about losing her. Next to my kids, she's my world. We never missed speaking at least three times a day and I saw her nearly every day. She loves my kids and gave me advice on raising them. She helped me decorate my house and shop for clothes. Mom knew everything and I relied on her judgment. Now all she does is stare at the TV. She doesn't talk at all." Melanie was sobbing.

"It must be excruciatingly painful to lose someone so close," I reflected her feelings.

"I can't go on without her. I feel like a baby. What'll I do? I'm dying with her." Melanie was devastated.

Melanie was still struggling with early separation-individuation developmental issues and was facing yet another separation from her. Only this was the final good-bye. Melanie was in a close state of fusion with her mother throughout her life, which left her feeling unprepared and incompetent to be her own person. She was overwrought with grief and anxiety about losing her mother who meant so much to her.

Upon further examination, we found that Melanie's husband made all the decisions in their marriage. If Melanie offered an opinion, Tom quickly shot her down, eroding what little self-confidence she had. We worked on the issue of independence. That meant challenging her husband and standing up to him. Before she married, Melanie worked as an office manager, delegating duties and keeping the office running efficiently. Yet, in her marriage, she lost her self and reverted to her childlike behavior with her mother.

With her mother's impending death, Melanie's arduous task was to relinquish her fantasy of merger with her. Mobilizing her former strengths, Melanie began to re-create her self as an independent, mature woman. Trying on her more assertive role with her husband shook the status quo. Complain as he might about Melanie's dependence on her mother, Tom was decidedly uncomfortable with her newfound independence. It collided with his wish to dominate his wife. Melanie persisted in her new path of growth and insisted that Tom join her in marital work.

Together, Melanie and Tom worked on a shared power relationship. In her time of sorrow, Melanie needed a strong shoulder to lean on, without the fear of sinking in and losing her self once again. Tom rose to the occasion and worked on granting Melanie the support and separateness she needed. Finding Melanie alone in their bedroom, sobbing grievously, he offered to comfort her. More often than not, Melanie felt solace by sobbing in his arms; yet, at times, she declined his offer, wishing to mourn alone. Respectful of her wishes, Tom quietly tiptoed away.

Muddled Emotions

Not everyone grieves in the same way. People with differing histories, personalities, and experiences mourn in various ways. Guilty feelings may resurface, with self- recriminations for some people exacerbating the mourning process. "Did I do enough? Perhaps I should have been there more for her? It's too late; now, I can never make amends," are some of the guilty reproaches I hear. Changing the past is impossible; however, drawing on past experience to enrich the soil for relating better in the future is possible.

Old unresolved problems with your parent gnaw at you. The opportunity to resolve these issues is lost, leaving you with a hopeless feeling. However, new opportunities, albeit not with the same person, will present themselves. Seizing the moment to act on new relationships in a different way can be empowering. Utilizing insight from prior experiences to build new bridges for a brighter tomorrow brings hope to dismal feelings.

One of the roughest relational issues that arise at death stems from mixed feelings adult children harbor about their parents. Experiencing unsatisfactory relationships with parents, adult children often hold onto love/hate feelings, as in Jason's case.

Love Laced with Loathing

"I hated him; he never had a good word for me. We fought over everything except the importance of family. I respected him for that, and my family is important to me. I didn't respect his attitudes and values. He was a bigot and the almighty dollar was his God. The funeral's tomorrow and I don't want to go." Jason's emotions were mixed.

"I can understand how you feel," I reflected.

"But he's my father, and a part of me loves the sonofabitch," he declared.

"Your love is laced with loathing," I interpreted his sentiments.

"I'm one mixed up dude. I guess I'll go to the funeral, but I won't stay long." Jason smiled. His split decision was a symbolic enactment of his muddled emotions.

Jason was in touch with the mixture of love and hate he felt for his father. Nevertheless, he was troubled by his equivocal love. Hate was close by, which would overcome Jason so that he lost sight of any positive attributes of his father. In effect, Jason either hated his father or loved him. In time, he learned to tolerate his ambivalent feelings so that he could keep a memory of his father as simply human, flawed no doubt, but with some admirable qualities.

Jason' s view of his self, similar to his view of his father, was either good or bad. A talented musician, Jason either bragged to me about a brilliant new song that was sure to get a Grammy or angrily shouted that he had torn up his "lousy" music in despair. We went to work integrating Jason's dichotomous feelings about his self as either absolutely perfect or totally defective. The process helped him mourn his father in a more authentic way, feeling the ache of his father's death more fully.

Unlike Jason, other people are unwilling to accept their ambivalent feelings. They jettison hate and reach for love. Hate, however, is biodegradable. It is absorbed into our systems and recycled into self-loathing. With hate turned inward, we reproach and torment ourselves. Without acknowledging our anger, it festers inside, complicating the mourning process, as in Mary Beth's case.

The Dark Side of the Moon

"I loved my mother unequivocally. She was a perfect mother. I coped well with her death as I felt it was a normal phase of life. My brother didn't get along with her. Oddly enough, he took her death much harder than I did. Now, three years later, he's fine, but I can't get out of bed. I cry all day and tear at my skin. I feel like a worthless, terrible person." Tears welled up as Mary Beth tried to maintain her equilibrium.

"You're in a deep agitated state of depression and you're torturing yourself," I commented.

"I am, but why now?" she asked.

"Maybe you've run away from some unwanted feelings," I suggested.

"Like what?" she questioned me.

"Like, maybe she wasn't so perfect and you have mixed feelings about her. You've told me your brother blamed your mother for criticizing both of you. Also, he remembered her harsh, punitive discipline. I believe he fought your mother tooth and nail. It doesn't sound like she was such an angel; you could well have buried some unwanted negative feelings. Ghosts are haunting you now." I cut to the chase.

"I remember how she hit us with a broom and threw things. Now that I think about it, I remember how, in rage, she held my hand to a hot stove till I wrested my hand from her iron grip. She was punishing me because I stole some money from her purse. It hurt so much, but I blamed myself. I shouldn't have done it; what I did was wrong. I felt that I deserved the punishment." Mary Beth was getting more real.

"So despite your mother's abuse, you protected the idealized image of your mother and blamed your self. Your rage was detoured, headed inside of you, and now you're feeling the effects. Depression is related to either loss or hate turned inward," I explained.

"I feel guilty about bad thoughts of her." She insisted on protecting the image of her dead mother, and blinding her self to the dark side of the moon.

"You tried to bury the traumatic abuse along with your anger and guilt. Unfortunately, your feelings are not at rest; they are causing havoc with you and complicating your mourning process."

Opening the portal to the traumatic past allowed a flood of sordid memories to gush in. Mary Beth needed a safe place and a witness to share her pain so that she could begin to heal. I was witness to her traumatic story and the accompanying feelings of helplessness, worthlessness, and distrust. Establishing a trusting relationship with me gave Mary Beth the courage to examine her fears of intimacy with others. She could see how her poignant history left her scarred and distrustful of new relationships. Rebuilding her trust and connection to others and feeling safe were some of the steps to her recovery. Mobilizing her strengths and talents to re-create her self were other steps. In time, the traumatic memories served as reminders of Mary Beth's strength to survive these pernicious events.

Like Mary Beth, adult children sometimes repress traumatic abuse in an effort to protect the image of the parent. The parent may have been all they had, and rather than fault him or her, they fault themselves. Repressing her feelings of hate and guilt, Mary Beth sank into a debilitating depression that was symptomatic of her punitive self-reproaches. Aside from depression, repressed feelings often manifest in physical symptoms, including chest pains and tremors.[3] Mary Beth's deep mourning began only after she arrived at these hurtful realizations.

Unlike hapless Jason and Mary Beth, many adult children are far more fortunate in their childhood relationships with parents. They have enjoyed close, loving relationships from early childhood right to the end, sharing a lifetime of joys and sorrows. Memories of compassion and caring through it all have left them with sanguine feelings. Does it make it easier? It all depends. Warm, cozy feelings often highlight the grievous loss of goodness. And it brings a different type of mourning, perhaps less complicated, but still replete with suffering.

Standing by helplessly while loved ones suffer debilitating transformations from robust individuals to shadows of their former selves is excruciatingly painful. When the long ordeal is finally over, some people may experience an unwelcome feeling of emancipation accompanied by guilt. Knowing that their loved ones are no longer suffering, coupled with feelings of liberation from their own burden, may bring a muddle of emotions—relief, elation, and sadness.

Losing a loved one with whom one enjoyed a favorable relationship may even result in anger. To their surprise, some adult children who have loved their parents dearly not only feel deep sorrow, but are often enraged with parents for leaving them. It does not seem reasonable. But since when are feelings reasonable? Worrying about your self and how you will manage without a beloved, close parent seems childish. Young children whose parents are divorcing inevitably cry out, "What will happen to me?" So, you are feeling like a young child. So what! You are feeling abandoned, and feelings of abandonment fly in the face of reality. All of these muddled emotions are troubling, but normal.

The Mourning Process

> Parting is such sweet sorrow.
>
> William Shakespeare

Aside from the morass of emotions, accepting the loss and adjusting to life without the person are part of the painful process of mourning. After parents depart, our memories live on—intimate moments, moments of conflict and stress, blissful moments, chaotic moments, happy moments, sad moments, and funny and serious moments. A lifetime of memories is all that remains to fill the dark, cavernous vacuum of death. Such is the sad stuff of mourning.

Mourning is a difficult and variable process. Everyone has their own style of mourning and their own timetable. For some people, mourning is not that severe in the moment, but it takes years to stop mourning. For other people, it is a natural but painful phase of life, and they are able to cease grieving faster than others.

Comparing your self to other family members is not a good idea. Each member of the family had a different relationship with parents, so their loss is experienced differently. Focusing on differences may create conflict. My great uncle Harry survived losses well, which may be one of the secrets to his longevity. He outlived two wives, numerous lady friends, and two sons. Not everyone is as hardy as Harry. Some people avoid the reality of loss and finality of death for a prolonged time. For other people, denial is short lived and simply an early stage of mourning.

When much of your life was organized around your parents' illness, you feel a void without them. Emotional and physical closeness has kept you filled in. You were the responsible adult caring for your helpless parent who needed you. You had a worthwhile purpose. Death brings emptiness, feelings of depletion, and worthlessness. Remember my discussion about role reversal in which you took on the adult role? You may not feel quite adult at this time, but rather, more like a fragile child abandoned by his or her parent. Crying, screaming, anguishing over the death of your parent, you feel like a small, bereft child. All of this is troubling, indeed, but an integral part of the mourning process.

Group Members Mourn

"When I awake, I think it's not really true; it's only a bad dream. Then reality sinks in and I cry bitterly. I miss her," Mark spoke sadly.

"I dreamed about him, that he and I were fishing in the bay. I caught the bigger fish and he was happy for me. It seemed so real when I woke up that I expected to see him knee deep in water. It took me awhile to orient myself." John joined Mark in mourning his loss.

"I keep thinking she's in the next room. Sometimes I go to check on her like I used to. It's weird." Katie looked dejected.

"I feel his presence with me, especially when I'm overcome with grief. He comforts me in his soothing reassuring way, and tells me I'm brave and that I'll be all right. I want to believe him," Kim wept quietly.

"The funeral helped me to accept that she really died." Hannah offered help.

"It helped me also. I didn't feel so alone, as friends and family cried with me." Roger amplified Hannah's offering.

"Gatherings of family and friends are good ways to connect with the living and the dead. Sometimes it's difficult to share deep feelings with family or close friends. Bereavement groups may be helpful. Internet sites provide anonymity, so you can pour your heart out and other people respond. Therapy also provides confidentiality, coupled with expertise. That may be the way to go. I believe going it alone is not advisable, but for some people, it's how they want to grieve." I offered some suggestions to the group.

"In the Jewish religion we sit shiva for one week. The family gets together and friends visit. They bring food, so the family is free to grieve. It feels good to be close to family, even if things weren't so hunky-dory before," Rachel informed the group.

"We had a wake, where family and friends got together. Then we met informally at each other's houses and shared good memories. I found it helped me to accept her death," Maria explained.

In my previous discussion of the relational self and the quantum physics, the notion of a cosmos where everyone is linked and connected to each other may bring solace. Are our souls connected through space and time—through infinity? Does Jung's theory of the collective unconscious have merit in light of the science of quantum physics? If so, what does it mean for our dead parents and us? How about our children and us after we die? Perhaps this intriguing theory may explain some of the unconscious identifications and connections to deceased parents. Indeed, examining quantum theory and the relational self at death raises a host of unanswered questions.

What is clearer is the comfort one derives by mourning the death of loved ones with others. Mourning in the company of other bereaved people, as in the preceding group, can be a bonding experience. Knowing that one is not alone, but linked and connected, as quantum theory suggests, provides solace at this heart-rending time. While death is a highly personal experience, it is nevertheless a universal event; hence we are all connected to each other in this way.

Speaking of unconscious connections, there is a new understanding of death that suggests the dying person may sense it. No matter the difficulty that close family and friends have in accepting that death is imminent, the dying person is likely to be aware of his or her impending deaths.[3] This uncanny phenomenon raises some issues.

Suddenly your parents are aware of their own death. As with other traumatic events, your parents may wish to talk about it, but remain silent out of fear they will upset you. In contrast, you try to protect them from the fear of dying. If so, whose fear is it really? Is it their fear or yours? Is avoidance your style of denying death?

Avoidance is not always the best thing for your parents. Not providing parents with a realistic prognosis undermines their autonomy. Indeed, reinforcing the person's autonomy emphasizes the fact that the person is still living. Your parents may wish to be informed so that they can prepare for death. Or they may not want to know. I would suggest that you take the lead from them, which involves tuning in to them and listening to them and to your heart.

If your parents broach the subject of their death, have a discussion at their pace and not yours. Too much information leads to feeling overwhelmed, whereas too little gives rise to feelings of insignificance. Like the "Goldilocks" effect—not too hot and not too cold—getting it just right is the ticket. Mirroring your parents emotions and merging with them may be all that is needed. You will be united by your feelings. Whether words or not are exchanged, empathy, concern, and love are bound to be comforting.

OUR OWN MORTALITY

> We should not forget that the minute we are born
> death becomes our companion.
> Gerd Fenchel[7]

> He not busy being born is busy dying.
> Bob Dylan

Is That All There Is?

The sorrowful death of parents is hard to bear for many reasons. One of the disquieting and ominous effects of our parents' mortality is fear of our own mortality. Are we ready to face it? Not so long ago we were young children enjoying a love affair with life; curious adolescents experimenting with life, ideologies, and meaning systems; young adults creating a career and searching for intimacy; married adults busy raising young families, with barely a moment to think about our selves, let alone our aging and mortality. Suddenly with the death of our parents, the dark specter of death hovers overhead. You may well ask yourself, "Is that all there is?" I would emphatically state, "no, not in the least." There is a lot of good living left. It depends on how you look at it.

While aging is humbling, with unmistakable limitations, aging can also point to new empowering paths for exploration. With greater wisdom, energies more directed, good and bad experience to draw from, this era can be productive and satisfying in new ways. Our youthful passions need not wane or dissipate; instead, with maturity, passions are more focused and plans more feasible. Many of us zeal-ously embark on new trajectories in careers and other meaningful endeavors. For some, it may be the opportune time to get involved in cultural activities, enroll in educational classes, take up tai chi chuan or the like—all of which we have put off. At midlife, with deceased parents and grown children, we can finally reap the benefits of our hard work over the years and enjoy our children, grandchildren, and greater leisure time. What is more, it is now our turn. Instead of delaying our pleasures, we have earned the right to enjoy them.

The inevitability of death down the road is, nevertheless, fearsome. Accepting death, however, is essential for a meaningful journey. In-deed, our mortality gives impetus to life. And if death is denied, so is life. In trembling and denying death, our fears manifest in constricted anxiety, depression, isolation, or meaningless exploits. Hence, energies and passions for creative, full living and loving go underground. In not living fully, people sentence themselves to self-imposed deaths.

Facing our mortality also provides an internal shift. We experience a change in our perspective on time, so that time lived shifts to time left to live.[8] The sobering new focus provides us with an urgent call to live life fully. Bearing in mind the truncated time left to live signals reallo-cation of energy and priorities. Making each moment count is the order of the new day.

Rehashing the past and constantly belaboring lost opportunities, bungled ones, or missed chances, are a waste of valuable time and energy. It only leaves us fearful of going forward. We cannot change the past, but we can learn from it to create better experiences in the present and future.

If we are reevaluating the past from a constructive place, we can improve on it. If our relationship to our selves and others was critical, superficial, or thoughtless, we need not despair. We can develop more profound, caring, intimate, and ultimately more gratifying ways of relating. What is more, revisiting prior satisfying experiences helps to mobilize creative forces for richer and more purposeful living. It is not too late to improve and to face the fear of impending death by choosing life.

What about Me?

Our mortality raises yet other fearsome questions. "Will I turn into my parent and be a burden to my children?" "Will I suffer like she did?" "Am I selfish to worry about my self at this mournful time?" These are normal worries that many people experience upon the death of their parents. Indeed, we are next, so it is expected that these fears will arise. The good news is you may well be met with a far different fate than your parents. New medical advances and alternative therapies increase the likelihood of better health and greater longevity and reduce the pain and suffering of illness.

Other questions may arise: "Who will take care of me?" "How will they fare without me?" Again it is expected that you would have these anxieties; we all do. Feeling abandoned and lost, you may worry that your children will suffer these feelings and you wish to spare them this pain. We may wish it were not so, but sorrow is inevitable; our children will likely suffer just as we have. Without sorrow and pain, they would not be the courageous, kind, fine adults that you wish them to be. Moreover, just as this time of sorrow will give you greater strength and endurance, when the time comes, it will do so for your children and loved ones.

Many of us worry about the uncertainty of our future. Others fear the effect of death on our children and loved ones, and worry about their welfare. Some of us fear both. I remember all too well the untimely death of my father and the long, agonizing death of my mother. Dwelling on your fate or the effects on your loved ones would not solve anything; it would just be paralyzing.

Embracing life and seizing the moment are the best antidotes for trepidation about the future. Nothing in life is certain, only death. Hence, it behooves us to live every precious moment of our lives with courage and meaning.

Notes

Sources are listed in numerical order of their first citation. Sources are sometimes cited multiple times in a chapter; similarly, more than one source is sometimes cited for a given fact or theory.

INTRODUCTION

1. Mitchell, S. A. (2002). *The Fate of Romance over Time.* New York: W. W. Norton.
2. Adler, H. O. (1998). Ministering to the dying mother: Reparative and psychodynamic opportunities for the female patient. In G. H. Fenchel (Ed.), *The Mother-Daughter Relationship: Echoes Through Time.* Northvale, NJ: Jason Aronson.

CHAPTER TWO

1. Merrill, D. M. (1997). *Caring for Elderly Parents.* Westport, CT: Auburn House.
2. Perricone, N. (2002). *The Perricone Prescription.* New York: Harper Resource.
3. Winnicott, D. W. (1971). Mirror role of mother and family in child development. In *Playing and Reality.* London: Tavistock.
4. Zohar, D. Z. (1990). *The Quantum Self.* New York: Quill/William Morrow.
5. Beebe, B. & Lachmann, F. M. (1998). Co-constructing inner and relational processes: Self and mutual regulation in infant research and adult treatment. *Psychoanalytic Psychology, 15,* 480–516.
6. Stern, S. (2002). The self as a relational structure. *Psychoanalytic Dialogues, 12(5),* 693–714.
7. Mitchell, S. A. (1993). *Hope and Dread in Psychoanalysis.* New York: Basic Books.
8. Klein, M. (1975). *Envy and Gratitude and Other Works, 1946–1963.* New York: Delacorte Press.
9. Mitchell, S. A. (2000). *Relationality: From Attachment to Intersubjectivity.* Hillsdale, NJ: The Analytic Press.
10. Jung, C. G. (1969). *The Archetypes and the Collective Unconscious.* Princeton, NJ: Bollingen Series/Princeton University Press.
11. Capra, F. (1985). *The Tao of Physics.* Boston: Shambhala.

12. Bohm, D. (1951). *Quantum Theory*. London: Constable.

13. Lasch, C. (1979). *The Culture of Narcissism*. New York: Warner Books.

14. Levin, J. & Levin, W. (1980). *Ageism: Prejudice and Discrimination Against the Elderly*. Belmont, CA: Wadsworth.

15. Palmore, E. (1997). Sexism and ageism. In J. M. Coyle (Ed.), *Handbook on Women and Aging*. Westport, CT: Greenwood Press.

16. Palmore, W. (1971). Attitudes towards aging as shown by humor. *Gerontologist, 11*, 181.

17. Cohen, E. S., & Kruschwitz, A. L. (1990). Old age in America represented in nineteenth and twentieth century popular sheet music. *Gerontologist, 30*, 245–354.

18. Becker, E. (1973). *The Denial of Death*. New York: Free Press, p. 66.

19. Bronte, L. (1993). *The Longevity Factor*. New York: HarperCollins.

20. Pollen, S. M. & Levine, M. (2003). *Second Acts*. New York: Harper Resource.

21. Rubinstein, R. (1986). *Singular Paths: Old Men Living Alone*. New York: Columbia University Press.

22. Doka, K. J. (1993). *Living with Life Threatening Illness*. New York: Lexington Books.

23. Kohut, H. (1977). *The Restoration of the Self*. New York: International University Press.

CHAPTER THREE

1. Cicerelli, V. G. (1981). *Helping Elderly Parents: The Role of Adult Children*. Boston: Auburn House.

2. Mitchell, S. A. (2002). *The Fate of Romance over Time*. New York: W. W. Norton.

3. Winnicott, D.W. (1960). *The Maturational Processes and the Facilitating Environment*. New York: International University Press.

4. Bromberg, P. (1996). Standing in the spaces: The multiplicity of self and the psychoanalytic relationship. *Contemporary Psychoanalysis, 32*, 509–535.

5. Gould, R. (1978). *Transformations: Growth and Change in Adult Life*. New York: Simon and Schuster.

6. Altschuler, J., Jacobs, S., & Shiode, D. (1985). Psychodynamic time-limited groups for adult children of aging parents. *American Journal of Orthopsychiatry, 33(3)*, 397–404.

7. Sherrel, K., Buckwallter, K. C., & Morhardt, D. (2001). Negotiating family relationships: Dementia care as a midlife developmental task. *Families in Society, 82(4)*, 383–392.

8. Fenchel, G. H. (1998). Introduction. In G. H. Fenchel (Ed.), *The Mother-Daughter Relationship: Echoes Through Time*. Northvale, NJ: Jason Aronson.

9. Cicirelli, V. G. (1990). Relationship of personal-social variables to belief in paternalism in parent caregiving situations. *Psychology and Aging, 5(3)*, 458–466.

10. Philips, L. R., Torres de Ardon, E., & Briones, S. G. (2000). Abuse of cargivers by care recipients: Another form of elder abuse. *Journal of Elder Abuse and Neglect, 12(3/4)*, 123–143.

11. Klein, M. (1975). *Envy and Gratitude and Other Works: 1946–1964*. New York: Delacorte Press.

CHAPTER FOUR

1. Abel, E. K. (1992). Parental dependence and filial responsibility in the nineteenth century. *Gerontologist, 32*, 519–526.

2. Klein, M. (1975). *Envy and Gratitude and Other Works: 1946–1964.* New York: Delacorte Press.

3. Neugarten, B. L. (1976). The awareness of middle age. In B. L. Neugarten (Ed.), *Middle Age and Aging.* Chicago: University of Chicago Press.

4. Blos, P. (1941). *The Adolescent Personality.* New York: Appleton-Century-Crofts.

5. Erikson, E. (1950). *Childhood and Society.* New York: W.W. Norton.

6. Merrill, D. (1997). *Caring for Elderly Parents.* Westport, CT: Auburn House.

7. Brainwaite,V. (1996). Women in the middle and family help to elder people. *The Gerontologist, 25,* 10–19.

8. Sally Bould (1997). Women and caregivers for the elderly. In J. M. Coyle (Ed.), *Handbook on Women and Aging.* Westport, CT: Greenwood Press.

9. Weisman, A. (1986). *The Coping Capacity: On the Nature of Being Mortal.* New York: Human Sciences Press.

10. West, R. L., Thorn, R. M., & Bagwell, D. K. (2003). Memory performance and beliefs as a function of goal setting and aging. *Psychology and Aging, 18(1),* 111–125.

11. Doka, K. J. (1993). *Living with Life Threatening Illness.* New York: Lexington Books.

CHAPTER FIVE

1. Frost, R. (2000). Fire and ice. In *American Poetry: The Twentieth Century, vol. 1.* New York: Literary Classics of the United States.

2. Bowlby, J. (1969). *Attachment and Loss. Vol. 1, Attachment.* New York: Basic Books.

3. Mitchell, S. A. (2002). *Can Love Last? The Fate of Romance over Time.* New York: W. W. Norton.

4. Klein, M. (1975). *Envy and Gratitude and Other Works, 1946–1964.* New York: Delacorte Press.

5. Bouklas, G. (1997). *Psychotherapy with the Elderly.* Northvale, NJ: Jason Aronson.

6. Hobbes, T. (1946). *Leviathon.* Oxford: Basil Blackwell.

7. Dollard, J., Miller, N., et al. (1939). *Frustration and Aggression.* New Haven: Yale University Press.

8. Sullivan, H. S. (1956). *Clinical Studies in Psychiatry.* New York: W. W. Norton.

9. Ainsworth, M. D. (1972). Attachment and dependency: A comparison. In J. L. Gewirts (Ed.), *Attachment and Dependency.* New York: Wiley & Sons.

10. Bowlby, J. (1980). *Attachment and Loss. Vol. 3, Sadness and Depression.* New York: Basic Books.

11. Cicerelli, V. G. (1981). *Helping Elderly Parents: The Role of Adult Children.* Boston: Auburn House.

12. Cohler, B. J. (1997). Fathers, daughters, and caregiving: perspectives from psychoanalysis and life-course social science. In J. M. Coyle (Ed.), *Handbook on Women and Aging.* Westport, CT: Greenwood Press.

13. Breuer, J., & Freud, S. (1893–95). Studies on hysteria. In J. Strachey (Ed. and Trans.), *The Standard Edition of the Complete Psychological Works of Sigmund Freud,* Vol. 2. London: Hogarth Press.

14. Adler, H. O. (1998). Ministering to the dying mother: Reparative and psychodynamic opportunities for the female patient. In G. H. Fenchel (Ed.), *The Mother-Daughter Relationship: Echoes through Time.* Northvale, NJ: Jason Aronson.

15. Donovan, M. W. (1998). Demeter and Persephone revisited: Ambivalence and separation in the mother-daughter relationship. In G. H. Fenchel (Ed.), *The Mother-Daughter Relationship: Echoes through Time.* Northvale, NJ: Jason Aronson.

16. Man Lai Kwan, C., Love, G. D., Ryff, C. D., & Essex, K. J. (2003). The role of self-enhancing evaluations in a successful life transition. *Psychology and Aging, 18(1),* 3–12.

CHAPTER SIX

1. Mitchell, S. A. (2002). *Can Love Last? The Fate of Romance over Time.* New York: W. W. Norton.

2. Klein, M. (1975). *Envy and Gratitude and Other Works, 1946–1964.* New York: Delacorte Press.

3. Winnicott, D. W. (1958). Hate in the countertransference. In *Collected papers: Through Paediatrics to Psycho-Analysis.* New York: Basic Books, pp. 194–203.

CHAPTER SEVEN

1. Mitchell, S. A. (2002). *Can Love Last? The Fate of Romance over Time.* New York: W. W. Norton.

2. Klein, M. (1975). *Envy and Gratitude and Other Works, 1946–1964.* New York: Delacorte Press.

3. Bollas, C. (1995). *Cracking Up: The Work of Unconscious Experience.* New York: Hill &Wang.

CHAPTER EIGHT

1. Merrill, D. M. (1997). *Caring for Elderly Parents.* Westport, CT: Auburn House.

2. Kohut, H. (1977). *The Restoraton of the Self.* New York: International Press.

3. Winnicott, D. W. (1965). *The Maturational Process and the Facilitating Environment.* New York: International Universities Press.

4. Aneschensel, C. S. (1986). Marital and employment role-strain, social suport, and depression among adult women. In S. E. Hobfoll (Ed.), *Stress, Social Support, and Depression among Adult Women.* Washington: Hemisphere, pp. 99–114.

5. Hirsch, B. J., & Rapkin, B. D. (1986). Multiple roles, social networks, and women's well-being. *Journal of Personality and Social Psychology, 51,* 1237–1247.

6. Monroe, S. M., Bromet, E. J., Connell, M. M., & Steiner, S. C. (1986). Social support, life events, and depressive symptoms: A 1-year prospective study. *Journal of Consulting and Clinical Psychology, 54,* 424–431.

7. Martire, L. M., Parris Stephens, M. A., & Townsend, A. L. (1998). Emotional support and well-being of midlife women: Role-specific mastery as a mediational mechanism. *Psychology and Aging, 13(3),* 396–404.

CHAPTER NINE

1. Sherrel, K., Buckwalter, K. C., & Morhardt, D. (2001). Negotiating family relationships: Dementia care as a midlife developmental task. *Families in Society, 82(4),* 383–392.

2. Mitchell, S. A. (1988). *Relational Concepts in Psychoanalysis.* Cambridge, MA: Harvard University Press.

3. Ogden, T. (1986). *The Matrix of the Mind.* Northvale, NJ: Jason Aronson.

CHAPTER TEN

1. Pinquart, M. & Sorensen, S. (2003). Differences between caregivers and noncaregivers in psychological health and physical health: A meta-analysis. *Psychology and Aging 18(2),* 250–267.

2. Cohler, B. J. (1997). Fathers, daughters and caregiving: Perspectives from psychoanalysis and life-course social science. In J. M. Coyle (Ed.), *Handbook on Women and Aging.* Westport, CT: Greenwood Press.

3. Cicerelli, V. G. (1991). Sibling relationships in adulthood. *Marriage and Family Review 16(3–4),* 291–310.

4. Merrill, D. M. (1997). *Caring for Elderly Parents.* Westport, CT: Auburn House.

5. Stoller, E. P., Forster, L. E., & Duniho, T. S. (1992). Systems of parent care within siblings' networks. *Research on Aging, 14,* 28–49.

6. Bould, S. (1997). Woman and caregivers for the elderly. In J. M. Coyle (Ed.), *Handbook on Women and Aging.* Westport, CT: Greenwood Press.

7. Klein, M. (1975). *Envy and Gratitude and Other Works, 1946–1964.* New York: Delacorte Press.

8. Doka, K. J. (1993). *Living with Life Threatening Illness.* New York: Lexington Books.

CHAPTER ELEVEN

1. Cicirelli, V. G. (1981). *Helping Elderly Parents.* Boston, MA: Auburn House.

2. Main, M. (1995). Recent studies in attachment: Overview with selected implications for clinical social work. In S. Goldberg, R. Muir, & J. Kerr (Eds.), *Attachment Theory.* Hillsdale, NJ: The Analytic Press.

3. Horowitz. A. (1978). Families who vary: A study of natural support systems of the elderly. Paper presented at the 31st Annual Scientific Meeting, Gerontological Society, Dallas, TX.

4. Adler, H. O. (1998). Ministering to the dying mother: Reparative and psychodynamic opportunities for the female patient. In G. H. Fenchel (Ed.), *The Mother-Daughter Relationship: Echoes through Time.* Northvale, NJ: Jason Aronson.

CHAPTER TWELVE

1. Cohler, B. J. (1997). Fathers, daughters, and caregiving. In In J. M. Coyle (Ed.), *Handbook on Women and Aging.* Westport, CT: Greenwood Press.

2. Kohut, H. (1977). *The Restoration of the Self.* New York: International Universities Press.

CHAPTER THIRTEEN

1. Doka, K. J. (1993). *Living with Life Threatening Illness.* New York: Lexington Books.

2. Bouklas, G. (1997). *Psychotherapy with the Elderly.* Northvale, NJ: Jason Aronson.

3. Kohut, H. (1977). *The Restoration of the Self.* New York: International Universities Press.

CHAPTER FOURTEEN

1. Finkelstein, N. (2002). Drones and chants. In *The Best American Poetry, 2002.* New York: Scribner.

2. Bowlby, J. (1980). *Attachment and Loss. Vol. 3. Loss, Sadness and Depression.* New York: Basic Book.

3. Doka, K. J. (1993). *Living with Life Threatening Illness.* New York: Lexington Books.

4. Siegler, A. L. (1998). Some thoughts on the creation of character. In G. H. Fenchel (Ed.), *The Mother-Daughter Relationship: Echoes through Time.* Northvale, NJ: Jason Aronson.

5. Mahler, M. S., Pine, F., & Bergman, A. (1975). *The Psychological Birth of the Human Infant.* New York: Basic Books.

6. Freud, S. (1917). Mourning and melancholia. *Standard Edition, 14,* 239–258.

7. Fenchel, G. H. (1998). Aging parents. In G. H. Fenchel (Ed.), *The Mother-Daughter Relationship: Echoes through Time.* Northvale, NJ: Jason Aronson.

8. Neugarten, B. L. (1967). The awareness of middle age. In B. L. Neugarten (Ed.), *Middle Age and Aging.* Chicago: University of Chicago Press.

Index

About the Author

FRANCES COHEN PRAVER, Ph.D., is a clinical psychologist and psychoanalyst working primarily with middle-aged people and couples caring for aging parents. She has appeared on television shows including *Good Morning America* and *The Phil Donahue Show*, and has lectured on trauma and traumatic stress in grand rounds at several hospitals.